SANJEEV KAPOOR'S
MICROWAVE COOKING made easy

In association with Alyona Kapoor

Popular Prakashan

POPULAR PRAKASHAN PVT. LTD.
35-C, Pt. Madan Mohan Malaviya Marg
Tardeo, Mumbai-400 034.

First Published 2004
First Reprint January 2004
Second Reprint April 2004

(3870)

ISBN - 81-7991-061-X

PRINTED IN INDIA
by Alert Packaging House Pvt. Ltd., 326, A to Z Industrial Estate
Ganpatrao Kadam Marg, Lower Parel, Mumbai 400 013 and
Published by
Ramdas Bhatkal
for Popular Prakashan Pvt. Ltd.
35-C, Pt. Madan Mohan Malaviya Marg
Tardeo, Mumbai-400 034.

Dedication

I dedicate this book to
my parents whose values and principles
have always been a tremendous source of
inspiration and strength to me.

Acknowledgements

A. I. Kazi
Aditi Mehta
Afsheen Panjwani
Anand Bhandiwad
Anil Bhandari
Brijesh Lohana
Capt. K. K. Lohana
Drs. Meena & Ram Prabhoo
Ganesh Pednekar
Grain of Salt, Kolkata
Harpal Singh Soklu
Jaideep Chaubal
Jijesh Gangadharan
Jyotsna & Mayur Dvivedi
Lohana Khaandaan
Meghana Samant
Namrata & Sanjiv Bahl
Neelima Acharya
Neena Murdeshwar
Puja & Rajeev Kapoor
Rajeev Matta
Rajneesh Sharma
Rutika Samtani
Shivani Ganesh
Smeeta Bhatkal
Sunit Purandare
Swapna Shinde
The Yellow Chilli, Jalandhar
The Yellow Chilli, Ludhiana
The Yellow Chilli, Amritsar
The Yellow Chilli, Delhi
The Yellow Chilli, Noida
Tripta Bhagattjee
Uma Prabhu
Vinayak Gawande

Author's Note

Superfast Microwave cooking saves time and labour. And nobody can deny the advantages of food being cooked minus smoke, grease and heat. This leaves the kitchen cool and clean at all times which is an unbelievable joy by itself. In this fast paced world it is a pleasure to present a collection of culinary creations that can be prepared in a jiffy!

There are two thoughts on microwave cooking. Experienced cooks are skeptical while inexperienced cooks are mystified! Most people who don't own one think a microwave oven is an expensive luxury. Those of us who have one, though, would find it difficult to live without it. Great advances have been made in the design and capabilities of microwave ovens since the demand for them first began in the sixties. With so many kinds of ovens available, both beginners and advanced cooks can find what best suits their particular needs.

A microwave oven is one appliance that can truly be termed user-friendly, for it can save you time, effort, energy, expense and washing up! They are hubs of activity in a lot of kitchens now. In this age and times when time is perhaps the most expensive commodity, microwave ovens are definitely a boon. With most women pursuing careers, there is very little time available to prepare goodies that will keep their families happy and content. Yet I found many misconceptions about the workings of a microwave oven. The most frequently asked questions are: Can we cook Indian food in this? Or can we bake a cake in this? Or can we make a gravy in this? The answer to all is, Yes! You can. And, believe me, it is not difficult. With a little ingenuity most traditional recipes can be adapted to microwave cooking once you have mastered the 'Microwave Language' and imbibed the 'tips' given in the book.

From popping popcorns to preparing jacket potatoes, making soggy foods crisp to re-heating beverages and food…microwave oven is, I am sure most of you would agree, a fantastic piece of technology. Now it is time to step ahead, with me, onto an interesting path of discovering the versatility of microwave cooking! Be it the Daily *Dal* or an Irish Coffee, be it a Smoky Fish *Kabab* or a Vegetable *Idli*, microwave cooking is THE thing to do!

The mechanics of microwave cooking are quite simple. And once grasped, they open the door to many exciting and memorable meals. This book brings for you the mechanics of microwave cooking that in turn will guide you through tested and recommended procedures for good results of every recipe.

Though the microwave oven is a boon to every busy woman's kitchen today, if not used with a bit of care and homework, you may land up overcooking or burning the dishes beyond repair. There is another point that causes fear among the new users of the microwave oven especially when the food sometimes explodes. However, like with most problems, this too has a solution. This book has many tips on safety and usage and it has all been done to make microwave cooking an enjoyable activity for you. Do go through the notes on microwave cooking specially prepared for you and included in the beginning of this book, which will put to rest any doubts or reservations you may have.

Another plus point is you can have fun while working, maybe whistle while you cook, for microwave cooking is a no-sweat, healthy start to a new chapter of cooking. Experimenting with the microwave may not bring the desired results in the first instance. But do not get disheartened and keep trying. The effort is worth it. Once you get the hang of it, you will be surprised how you ever managed without it.

A lot of people are under the misconception that a microwave can perform almost any task related to cooking. Let's be honest – it cannot. For example, it cannot fry you a *samosa* or a *dosa*. It also cannot give you that beautiful golden brown crust. But then a pressure cooker cannot grill a luscious *kabab*. So also does the gas stove have its limitations. It cannot bake a cake; you need an oven. Yet when you count the numerous ways in which a microwave oven can make life easier, it is definitely worth every rupee that you pay for it.

Numerous people have often asked me whether it is safe to cook in a microwave oven. Obviously they have been thinking about the controversial reports regarding this mode of cooking. However, there are no research results to back such claims even in the developed countries where most people are totally dependent on microwave ovens for their daily meals. On the contrary, since food gets cooked in its own juices it is full of natural aroma, colour and texture. Nutrients are preserved because food is not exposed to heat for long periods. Besides, microwave ovens are non-ionising appliances, they do not change the physical and chemical properties of food, they only heat it up. Microwaves are just another form of energy and are totally safe.

All the recipes in this book provide for four portions. The portion size has been set keeping in mind that they will form part of a menu which will have other complementary dishes and will be shared by a group of people. Care has been taken to include dishes that will cover all the courses from starters to desserts.

So here's to microwave cooking that keeps the taste and nutrient content hale 'n hearty for a healthy you!

Contents

Breads & Rice

Desserts

Beverage

Annexure

Basics of Microwave

Although microwave ovens have been around for many years, they still evoke more confusion than confidence in novices as well as in experienced chefs and housewives. One has to accept the fact that at first glance it is not an easily understandable mode of cooking specially when we are coming from a closed mindset of conventional cooking techniques. Let's give you a few basic concepts and you will be ready to explore the untreaded path and enjoy cooking speedily in a less messy way, while preserving the inherent goodness of the food.

A microwave oven has a magnetron vacuum tube which converts electrical energy into high frequency microwaves. Once produced they:

- are reflected by metal surfaces, therefore they are safely contained in the oven cavity. For the same reason metal vessels are not used for holding food in the microwave oven;

- can pass through a substance without changing it. It can pass through materials like china, glass, pottery or wood without heating them. This explains why these when used in a microwave do not become hot. They become hot only through conduction of heat from the food therein; and

- can be absorbed. They are absorbed by moisture in foods, causing the food molecules to vibrate rapidly. This vibration causes friction between the food molecules and the result is intense heat which cooks the food. The food molecules vibrate at the rate of multi millions of times per second accounting for the speed of microwave cooking.

Combination microwave ovens cook using microwave energy and conventional oven heat simultaneously, although if desired they can be operated by microwave alone or convection alone or in tandem or in some cases with a grill. Usually basic combination ovens offer a minimum of three cooking methods.

- **Microwave only:** This mode of cooking can be used alone in exactly the same way as you would use a basic microwave oven. This is effectively used for cooking soups, steamed type fish dishes, vegetables, fruits, rice, pasta, pulses, steamed puddings, sauces and eggs.

⧇ **Convection only:** This mode of cooking is the same as that used in a conventional oven, but it may be fan assisted or turbo charged in some cases. It is temperature controlled usually from 100° C to 250° C. Used for baking small cakes, biscuits, meringues, choux pastries and small crisp pastry items.

⧇ **Combination only:** This is the mode where the microwave and convection systems operate together to give fast cooking results with traditional browning and crisping. You simultaneously get microwave energy and re-circulating hot air, from a cold start. The microwave energy provides rapid cooking whereas the hot air gives a baked, browned or roasted appearance. Used for cooking small and large cuts of meat, poultry and game; for cooking fish either whole or in pieces; vegetable gratins; pastry pies; sweet and savoury pastry dishes; hot puddings; cakes; breads and tea-breads; browned pasta dishes like lasagne etc.

Combination microwave ovens do tend to be more expensive and require more energy than conventional microwave ovens but they are able to brown and crisp meats while preserving their juiciness, permit baking and can speed up cooking time when a number of dishes are to be cooked.

Combi oven functions in various modes. You can just use it as Microwave with 1000 W output. Convection oven has a range of 100°C to 250°C, a pre heating facility – has cube heater (top, bottom, rear) plus convection fan. Mostly Grill mode comes in three forms: Grill (TOP) also called browning grill; Grill (BOTTOM) also called crispy grill and Grill (TOP & BOTTOM) also called double grill. Use TOP for browning (kababs) and melting cheese, BOTTOM for making things crisp (pizza base) and TOP & BOTTOM for making things which should be crisp as well as brown on top (pizza).

Then you have COMBI mode. Used generally for:

1. Convection + Microwave,
2. Convection + Grill (BOTTOM) + Microwave,
3. Convection + Grill (TOP & BOTTOM),
4. Grill (TOP) + Microwave and
5. Grill (TOP & BOTTOM) + Microwave.

Select proper mode as per the dish. It will come to you with experience. The power consumption in Combi mode goes upto 2800W.

Depending on your cooking needs and available space, choose an oven with an appropriate size and power. Microwaves usually range from about 0.4 cubic feet to 1.8 cubic feet and from 500 to 1100 watts of power. If the microwave will be used only for heating coffee, making popcorn, defrosting frozen food, or warming leftovers, a smaller unit should suffice. For more serious cooking or for a large family, you'll probably need a larger oven. Higher wattage enables faster cooking. Microwave recipes are usually written for about 800 watts of power, so you can check and see how long it will take to make your favourite foods. Large capacity but under-powered microwaves can be very frustrating to use.

Most microwave ovens offer a built-in turntable. Note that turntables reduce the available size for the dish. A useful feature is being able to turn the turntable on and off, so large dishes can still be cooked. Another solution is the use of a stirrer that redistributes the microwave energy in every direction, resulting in even heating.

Today, almost all microwaves use touch pad controls instead of a rotary dial. Thanks to the common use of microchips, many microwave ovens can be programmed to perform multiple tasks, for example to auto-start cooking at a chosen time, set power levels, or allow multi-step cooking.

Most microwaves have a clock that displays either the actual time or the cooking time. Additional features sometimes offered are auto-defrost and auto-reheat that automatically set the time and power levels based on the food weight and type, extra kitchen timer, one-touch buttons for popcorn or drinks, and one-more-minute button that adds time but leaves other settings unchanged. High-end units offer other convenient built-in features like temperature and moisture sensors that can prevent overcooking.

Here's hoping that this will help you to use your Microwave oven to its maximum potential!

Myths and Realities

To microwave or not to microwave is the question! Here are some facts that compare the microwave method of cooking with conventional modes

MYTH	REALITY
Microwave is good only for reheating.	Apart from cooking all types of vegetarian and non-vegetarian foods, a microwave oven is also extremely useful for defrosting, boiling, baking, reheating etc.
Food does not taste as delicious as compared to food cooked conventionally.	On the contrary, food is cooked in its own juices and as a result it is full of natural aroma, colour and texture.
Indian food cannot be cooked in a microwave oven.	The microwave oven can cook and how! Try out Indian foods like *idli, biryani, kheer,* curry, *kabab* and what have you.
Microwave ovens emit radiation which is harmful to health, so much that it could cause cancer.	Microwave ovens are non-ionising appliances, they do not change the physical and chemical properties of food but they only heat the same. Microwaves when exposed to the food get completely absorbed. This helps in heating/cooking the food. The heat is generated by causing friction between the microwaves and the food molecules. The microwaves get completely converted into heat and there is nothing left behind in the food. Microwaves are just another form of energy and are totally safe.

The running cost of a microwave oven is expensive.	Though the electricity tariff differs from place to place, it has been generally observed that the cost of using a microwave oven on a regular basis is on par with the cost of using traditional fuel like gas. Besides this, microwave cooking requires very little oil and spices compared to conventional cooking, so there is evidently some cost cutting!
Microwave ovens are very complicated to use.	A microwave oven is very easy to operate. All it requires is a little practice. It is so simple that even children and the elderly can comfortably use it.

Equipment for the Microwave Oven

Here's a list of utensils that can be used for microwave cooking. And yes, it might not lead to unnecessary shopping! So read on...

A microwave oven works because the microwaves pass through the food container and into the food. Microwaves can pass through many things but not through metal. This includes twist ties, which cause arcing. They can pass easily through most kinds of plastic, paper, glass and any pottery or china without metal trim, paint or glaze. The range of equipment that can be used in the microwave oven is more extensive than that can be used in conventional oven cooking.

- For short cooking operations where temperatures are not excessively high, paper cookware, plastic cookware, greaseproof paper, absorbent kitchen paper, paper and linen napkins and fine china can be used.
- For longer cooking operations where temperatures are high it is worthwhile investing in a good comprehensive range of heatproof glassware or microwave cookware. Ceramic wares can also be used but make sure that they don't have any metallic rim as they may cause arcing. Food items containing high proportion of fat and sugar should not be cooked in glass utensils, otherwise they can be used commonly.
- Microwave polyethylene bags and microwave-safe cling films are also good for general use but must be thrown away after use.

NOTE

Do not use melamine in the microwave oven - it absorbs enough microwave energy to cause charring or burning which is irreversible. Paper towels and cardboard can also be used provided they don't have any staple pins in them. Wood items can be used in the microwave oven but not for a long time.

CONTAINER SHAPES

This is an important factor to be noted. Dishes must be half or three-quarters filled depending on the liquid content of the food. If the dish is too small, the food will boil over and if the dish is too large the thick curry will spread out and overcook. Shallow vessels make cooking faster. Cakes, chicken, meat and rice dishes cook well in large bottomed vessels while round dishes are ideal for cooking vegetables and curry dishes. Any foods, which need to be boiled in the microwave like pasta, rice, jams and some soups or casseroles, should be put into a dish, which seems much too big for the quantity. This allows the mixture to rise high on the sides of the dish (and it will!) without spilling over and messing up the oven.

TESTING POTTERY AND CHINA FOR USE IN THE MICROWAVE

Metal glazes are not always obvious. While it is easy to see gold lines in a pattern, many metals are ingredients in pottery glazes to give different colours, including reds, blues, greens and browns. Usually the amount of metal in a coloured glaze will not be enough to cause problems, but sometimes the clay itself contains high amounts of iron, especially dark coloured or speckled clays. If you want to see whether pots or plates you already have are suitable for microwave oven, try this simple test. Put the empty dish into the microwave on HIGH for 60 seconds. If the dish becomes noticeably warm or hot it has a high metal content and should not be used in the microwave. Do not leave the microwave on for longer than 60 seconds without any food or water in it. The waves then bounce back into the magnetron and can eventually burn it out.

Metal skewers with wooden handles can be used in the microwave provided the food is packed tightly together leaving no metal exposed. Wooden skewers are anyday better.

As microwave cooking is gaining popularity day by day, many manufacturers now make ranges of special microwave cookware. They are generally made of ceramic glass or thermoplastic. Both can be used in the conventional oven too though thermoplastic cookware can be used only upto a certain moderate temperature. The range of dishes is expanding from general cooking dishes to specific recipe or item oriented ones like cake moulds, egg poachers, steamers, *idli*-maker, omelet-maker, microwave saucepans! It makes an interesting economic sense to go in for such dishes which will also go in the freezer i.e. you cook, serve and store in the same dish!

WHAT'S AVAILABLE IN THE MARKET

Few of the microwave fare available in the market are:

Disposable cookware: Plastic, polythene, treated paper board, greaseproof paper, microwave-safe cling film etc.

Browning dishes: Made of glass ceramic substance with a special coating, which attracts and absorbs microwave energy. Food in contact with this will get more heat and browning effect will show.

Microwave pressure cooker: Reduces cooking time upto 35%. It cooks food in microwave under gentle pressure, sealing in moisture and nutrients.

Steamer baskets: Expandable to fit a good range of dishes. Elevates the food item above the water for steaming.

Microwave splatter screen: It keeps the splatters of soups, sauces etc. in while allowing steam to vent out through a specially designed grid.

Microwave potato baker: A device which positions potatoes in a ring pattern and at an angle for maximum and even microwave absorption.

Microwave cooking pouch holder: It's for holding safely the frozen cook-in-the-bag ready meals during microwave cooking. Remember to pierce holes on the top of the pouch.

Microwave ladle, whisk, spoon: They can be left in oven cavity during cooking. Take care that they do not restrict any turntable action by catching on the walls or ceiling.

Microwave stacking rings and shelf organizers: Thermoplastic rings and shelves used to separate plates or dishes when cooking or reheating food resulting in optimum utilization of oven cavity.

SOME SPECIAL THINGS

Now the food industry is developing special microwave packaging for frozen or chilled foods. You can see departmental stores and your grocery shop stacking special microwave chips, pizza, popcorns and batter-coated products for microwave-only heating. They have a special packaging that activates and utilizes microwave energy to give a particular heating effect.

Combination & Convection:

In combi mode it's better to use dishes meant for microwave like glass and ceramics while for purely convection, metal cookware can be used with confidence.

Frequently Asked Questions

It's good to ask questions because they are the answers to almost all problems. Here are some Frequently Asked Questions that could be the Troubleshooters!

TIMING IS THE KEY

How do I calculate the cooking time while adapting a conventional recipe for the microwave oven?

As a rough guide most foods will require approximately a quarter to one third of the conventional cooking time. If unsure, always underestimate the time needed, check the result and continue cooking if needed. More the food, longer the cooking time. When doubling a recipe, increase the cooking time by half and check the result.

COVERING CAN BE A SAVIOUR

I find it confusing while using a microwave oven: to cover or not to cover?

Cover foods for the same reasons as in conventional cooking: to retain moisture, speed up cooking and to help tenderise foods. Use a vented lid for foods with a high liquid content, such as soups, to allow steam to escape and prevent the liquid boiling over. You can use cling film to cover. Ensure to pierce it all over. Covering food with a sauce has the same effect as using a lid when cooking meat or poultry. Do not cover foods, like cakes and crumbles, on which you desire a dry finish or for quick-cooking items such as scrambled eggs and for foods which need frequent stirring like sauces and custards.

STIRRING SPEEDS UP

Is it a must to stir foods while cooking?

Food nearest the sides of the dish cooks faster than that at the centre, so stirring will speed up its cooking time and ensure even cooking. Particularly sensitive foods, such as scrambled eggs and sauces, need frequent stirring during cooking.

TURNING IS A MUST

Arranging food and turning over while it is cooking seems to be the secret of even cooking.

When thawing, heating or cooking large items, such as a whole chicken, start off by placing the food upside down. Turn it over half way through the required time.

Arranging is necessary since the food at the outer edges of the turntable or dish generally receives more microwave energy than that at the centre, so place thicker or larger portions of food at the outer edge. Rearranging is essential with food that cannot be stirred since it moves the food and encourages even cooking. Move the food from the centre of the dish to the outside and vice versa.

STACKING CAN BE HELPFUL

I have seen some people stack containers to save time. Is it the done thing?

Stacking can be done when re-heating foods in flat-topped containers, plated meals with rigid plate covers or plates separated by plate rings. For even heating arrange the plates or containers so that thicker foods such as jacket potatoes are evenly distributed in the stack, e.g. with the potato on the lower plate (or container) on the opposite side to the potato on the upper plate (or container). Stack no more than two plates or containers for best results.

KEEPING FOOD HOT IS EASY

Food cooked in microwave oven seems to cool faster than that made traditionally. Why? And how can we insulate the dishes?

Food cooked in the microwave cools more quickly than food cooked conventionally because in conventional cooking the container becomes hot and transfers heat to the food, whereas in microwave cooking the opposite is true. When microwaving times are short and the dish does not become hot, food will cool very quickly after the standing time. This is easily overcome with some simple insulating ideas i.e. placing the dish in a basket or quilted casserole or wrapping it in colourful napkins after microwaving.

FOILING THE ALUMINIUM COVER

Aluminium foil to cover dishes in microwave ovens is taboo. Why?

Microwaves can pass through most materials such as china, glass, plastic and paper. They cannot pass through metal. They are reflected by it. It is therefore advisable not to use foil in a microwave as it may cause sparking which may damage the walls of the microwave. Foil can be extremely useful for keeping food hot when it is out of the microwave but food must never be returned to the microwave wrapped or covered in foil. Only small portions of food, which are likely to be scorched, can be covered with foil for a brief time.

UNDERSTANDING STANDING TIME

Is it important to pay attention to standing time given in the recipes?

Yes, observing standing times can help you cook better! After a food has reached the end of the required cooking time (and the oven has automatically switched off) it will continue to cook by the conducted heat still trapped in the food. To ensure that a food does not overcook with this "additional" energy effect, a standing time of a few minutes should be observed. In most cases this is only two to three minutes but can be upto fifteen minutes for large baked cakes and roasts. In the case of roasts this standing time is best carried out under foil.

Microwave Tips

Some neat tips to use your microwave oven more effectively and efficiently.

- ❯❯ Always remove the lid or cover from hot microwaved food by lifting it from the end of the dish away from you to prevent being scalded by the steam.

- ❯❯ To dry herbs for storage place the sprigs between paper towels and microwave until the herbs can be crumbled.

- ❯❯ To blanch almonds bring one cup water to a boil for about two to three minutes on HIGH (100%), add nuts, cook on HIGH (100%) for one minute and drain. The skins should slip off easily.

- ❯❯ To roast coconut spread it in an even layer on a plate and heat on MEDIUM (70%) for one minute, tossing twice with a fork. Leave to cool and store in airtight jars.

- ❯❯ To roast nuts, spread the nuts on a ceramic plate adding salt or any other masala to taste if so desired/required and cook on HIGH (100%) for two minutes. Stir twice while microwaving and do not allow to brown too much. They will darken as they cool. Serve after five minutes.

- ❯❯ To roast *papads* brush them lightly with oil on both sides and cook for thirty seconds on HIGH (100%).

- ❯❯ To crisp biscuits, nuts, chips etc, place them on a plate and heat on HIGH (100%) for one minute and allow it to stand for five minutes.

- ❯❯ To warm and freshen breads, rolls or cakes wrap them in paper towels and heat on HIGH (100%) for fifteen to twenty seconds.

- ❯❯ To warm *chapatis*, wrap them in a napkin or in a paper towel and heat on HIGH (100%) for thirty seconds.

- ❯❯ To make breadcrumbs for toppings and coatings, cut bread in cubes and microwave for five minutes on HIGH (100%). Allow it to stand for five minutes. Cool and crush in a blender or a food processor and store.

- ❯❯ If you have forgotten to soak pulses, lentils, beans overnight, do not despair. Cover them with water in a large bowl and heat on HIGH (100%) for about ten minutes to bring to a boil. Allow the pulses to boil for two more minutes and then leave to stand for one hour. The pulses will cook faster.

- To peel tomatoes easily place them with one cup water, uncovered, on HIGH (100%) for two to three minutes or till boiling. Then place in a bowl containing cold water. Remove the skin.

- To cook potatoes place them in a dish half filled with water. Cover and cook on HIGH (100%) for around five minutes and then allow standing time of five minutes. Drain, cool and peel. If you only need a couple of potatoes, you can cook them without water also.

- To let air circulate underneath breads, cakes and pastry shells, place them on a rack or inverted saucer. This allows the base to cook more evenly.

- Always slightly undercook the dish a little bit since food cooked in the microwave oven will cook further during standing time. Standing time is that period when the dish is kept covered to finish the cooking process since it uses up the remaining heat to cook further.

- Food like potatoes and sausages etc. should be pierced with a pointed instrument like fork or tip of knife to avoid bursting of steam build up.

- Excess juice released from food during cooking can slow down cooking process as it will attract microwave energy. Remove excess juice during cooking and reintroduce later if required.

- For even cooking, arrange items in a ring pattern so that they receive equal amounts of energy.

- If items are of uneven size then the thicker items should be positioned at the outer edge of the dish where they will receive more energy.

- For even results, cook, as far as possible, in round dishes.

- Dense food takes more time to cook.

- Cooking time is related to the quantity of food to be cooked, more the food, the longer is the cooking time.

- High fat and sugar items will generally cook faster than the water-based products as fat and sugar absorb microwave energy faster.

- While reheating food, cover with a lid to retain moisture. Place an absorbent napkin for dry items that run the risk of becoming soggy. Let the reheated food stand in the microwave for sometime before removing it.

- Do not boil egg in the microwave oven. Do not reheat boiled egg in microwave even if the shell is removed. For poaching/steaming/frying preparations, break eggs, pierce the yolk and then cook.

- Whenever you use Combination mode always remember that the container you use will get heated. So, keep oven gloves handy !

SANJEEV KAPOOR'S

MICROWAVE
COOKING made easy

Minestrone Soup

INGREDIENTS

Carrot	1 medium sized	Fresh basil leaves	10-12
Potato	1 medium sized	Tomatoes	4 medium sized
Zucchini	1 medium sized	Oil	1½ tbsps
Garlic	6-8 cloves	Vegetable stock*	3 cups
Onion	1 medium sized	Tomato puree	½ cup
Green peas (shelled)	¼ cup	Macaroni	2 tbsps
Celery	1 inch stalk	Salt	to taste
Leek	½ stalk	White pepper powder	½ tsp
French beans	3-4	Parmesan cheese (grated)	½ cup

METHOD OF PREPARATION

1. Peel, wash and cut carrot, potato and zucchini into half inch sized cubes. Peel, wash and chop garlic and onion. Wash green peas.

2. Wash and cut celery and leek into half inch sized pieces. String, wash and cut French beans into half inch sized pieces. Wash and roughly chop half the basil leaves.

3. Give a superficial cross-cut with a sharp knife on top of the tomatoes. Blanch tomatoes in sufficient water in a deep microwave bowl for two minutes on Microwave HIGH (100%) and transfer them immediately into a bowl of cold water. Peel the skin, cut into half and remove seeds and cut further into half inch sized pieces.

4. In a large microwave casserole heat oil (preferably olive oil) for three minutes on Microwave MEDIUM (70%). Remove, add garlic, onion, carrot, leek and celery and cook for six minutes on Microwave HIGH (100%), stirring occasionally.

5. Add French beans, zucchini, potato, green peas, tomato puree and tomatoes. Add remaining half of the fresh basil leaves broken by hand, vegetable stock and cook for eight minutes on Microwave HIGH (100%). Add the macaroni, salt and white pepper powder, cover and cook on Microwave HIGH (100%) for five minutes.

6. Garnish with fresh basil strips and grated parmesan cheese. Serve piping hot.

NOTE

*Refer page no. 124 for the recipe of vegetable stock.

CHEF'S TIP

Instead of leek you can use spring onions.

Garden Vegetables & Almond Soup

INGREDIENTS

Broccoli	¼ small sized	Fresh basil	4 leaves
Carrot	1 medium sized	Almonds	20-25
Spring onions	2	Oil	1 tbsp
Fresh mushrooms	5-6	Vegetable stock*	4 cups
Lettuce leaves	3-4	Salt	to taste
Garlic	3 cloves	Thyme	a pinch
Corn kernels	¼ cup	Soy sauce	1 tsp

METHOD OF PREPARATION

1. Wash and cut the broccoli into medium sized florets. Peel, wash and cut carrot into half inch sized cubes. Wash and chop spring onion bulbs and four-five greens. Wash and slice mushrooms. Wash and shred lettuce. Peel and chop garlic. Wash corn kernels. Wash and shred basil leaves.

2. Place almonds with sufficient water in a deep bowl and cook on Microwave HIGH (100%) for three minutes. Drain, peel and cut into slivers and keep it aside.

3. Put oil, carrot, vegetable stock, spring onion, garlic, corn kernels, salt and almond slivers in a deep casserole and cook on Microwave HIGH (100%) for seven minutes.

4. Add broccoli, mushrooms, spring onion greens, thyme, basil, lettuce leaves, soy sauce and cook further on Microwave HIGH (100%) for five minutes.

5. Serve piping hot.

NOTE

*Refer page no. 124 for the recipe of vegetable stock.

Fresh Tomato Soup

INGREDIENTS

Tomatoes	8 medium sized	Oil	½ tbsp
Garlic	6 cloves	Butter	1 tbsp
Carrot	1 medium sized	Bay leaf	1
Celery	2 inch stalk	Salt	to taste
Onion	1 medium sized	Sugar	1 tsp
Parsley	a few sprigs	Cream	¼ cup
Peppercorns	4-6	Bread Croutons	12-16

METHOD OF PREPARATION

1. Wash and cut tomatoes into quarters. Peel, wash and chop garlic. Peel, wash and cut carrots into roundels. Wash and chop celery. Peel, wash and slice onion. Wash and chop parsley. Crush peppercorns.

2. Put oil, butter, onion, carrot, celery, garlic, bayleaf in a large microwave bowl and cook for five minutes on Microwave HIGH (100%).

3. Add quartered tomatoes, salt, sugar and three cups of water and cook covered on Microwave HIGH (100%) for twenty-five minutes.

4. Let it cool slightly. Blend in a blender till smooth. Add crushed peppercorns and cook further on Microwave HIGH (100%) for five minutes.

5. Stir in cream and garnish with chopped parsley. Serve piping hot with bread croutons.

NOTE

For making bread croutons, cut two bread slices into half inch sized squares. Put on a microwave plate and cook on Microwave HIGH (100%) for ten minutes. It can be grilled too in a Combi oven for the same duration.

Tom Yum Kung

INGREDIENTS

Prawns .... 20 small sized	Lime leaves 6
Mushrooms 5-6	Salt .... to taste
Fresh coriander leaves .... A few sprigs	Fish sauce .... 2 tbsps
Green or fresh red chillies 4	Thai red curry paste* .... 2 tsps
Lemon grass .... 4 inch stalk	Lemon juice .... 3 tbsps

METHOD OF PREPARATION

1. Remove head and shells of prawns, de-vein and wash them thoroughly under running water.

2. Clean, wash and slice the mushrooms. Clean, wash and chop the coriander leaves. Remove stems and wash chillies. Wash lemon grass and lime leaves.

3. Place the head and shells in a microwave bowl with four to five cups of water. Bruise lemon grass stems, two lime leaves and two green (or red) chillies in a mortar or tear them with hand and add to the pan. Add salt, cover and cook for fifteen minutes on Microwave HIGH (100%). Strain the stock.

4. Slice the remaining chillies into fine roundels and reserve for garnish.

5. In a large microwave casserole add the stock, sliced mushrooms and prawns. Cover and cook (simmer) for eight minutes on Microwave MEDIUM (70%) or until the prawns are pink and cooked.

6. Stir in the fish sauce, red curry paste and lemon juice to make the soup sharp and tangy. Adjust the seasoning.

7. Pour into a serving bowl and garnish with green or fresh red chilli roundels and the whole lime leaves. Serve piping hot.

NOTE
*Refer page no. 82 for the recipe of Red Curry Paste (Prawns in Thai Red Curry Sauce).

Chicken Shorba

INGREDIENTS

Chicken (boneless)	100 gms	Oil	1 tbsp
Onion	1 medium sized	Cumin seeds	½ tsp
Garlic	4-5 cloves	Chicken stock*	4 cups
Fresh coriander leaves (optional)	2 tbsps	Salt	to taste
Peppercorns	5-6	Cream	¼ cup

METHOD OF PREPARATION

1. Clean, wash and cut chicken into half inch sized cubes. Peel, wash and slice onion. Peel and chop garlic. Clean, wash and chop coriander leaves. Crush peppercorns.

2. Put oil, cumin seeds and garlic in a large microwave casserole and cook on Microwave HIGH (100%) for one minute. Add hot chicken stock, chicken pieces, crushed peppercorns, salt and cook, covered, further on Microwave HIGH (100%) for twelve minutes.

3. Stir in the cream. Pour into individual cups, garnish with chopped coriander leaves and serve hot.

NOTE
*Refer page no. 125 for the recipe of chicken stock.

Sichuan Hot Soup

INGREDIENTS

Chicken (boneless) .... 100 gms
Carrot .... 1small sized
Cabbage .... ¼ small sized
Dried black mushrooms 4
Beancurd .... 50 gms
Peppercorns 6-8
Capsicum .... ½ medium sized
French beans 4-5

Spring onions 2
Cornstarch .... 3 tbsps
Salt .... 1 tsp
Vinegar .... 3 tbsps
Sugar .... 1 tsp
Red chilli paste .... 1 tbsp
Chicken stock* .... 3 cups

METHOD OF PREPARATION

1. Clean, wash and cut chicken into very small pieces.

2. Peel, wash and grate carrot. Wash and shred cabbage. Clean, wash and chop mushrooms. Cut the beancurd into one centimetre sized squares. Crush peppercorns.

3. Wash, de-seed and chop capsicum. Wash, string and chop French beans. Wash and finely chop spring onion bulb and three-four greens.

4. Dissolve the cornstarch in quarter cup of water, stir in salt, vinegar, sugar, red chilli paste and peppercorns.

5. Put carrot, cabbage, spring onion bulb, mushroom, capsicum, French beans, chicken and chicken stock in a deep microwave bowl. Cover and cook on Microwave HIGH (100%) for eight minutes.

6. Add the cornstarch mixture and beancurd and cook uncovered on Microwave HIGH (100%) for five minutes.

7. Check seasoning and serve piping hot garnished with spring onion greens.

NOTE
*Refer page no. 125 for the recipe of chicken stock.

Nachos

INGREDIENTS

Crisp corn chips 16-20	Capsicum .... 1 medium sized
Processed cheese (grated) .... ¾ cup	Peppercorns 5-6
For the salsa sauce	Dry oregano .... ¼ tsp
Tomatoes .... 2 large sized	Sweet chilli sauce* .... 2 tbsps
Onion .... 1 medium sized	Salt .... to taste
Garlic .... 2-3 cloves	

METHOD OF PREPARATION

1. Wash, halve, de-seed and finely chop tomatoes. Peel, wash and chop onion. Peel and crush garlic. Wash, halve, de-seed and chop capsicum. Crush peppercorns.

2. Combine these with the rest of the ingredients and let the salsa sauce stand at room temperature for an hour before use.

3. Arrange the corn chips on a microwave plate, top it up with the salsa sauce and grated cheese. Cook, uncovered, on Microwave HIGH (100%) for two minutes.

4. Serve immediately, otherwise the corn chips will turn soggy.

> **NOTE**
> *Refer page no. 93 for the recipe of Sweet Chilli Sauce.

> **CHEF'S TIP**
> A topping made with white sauce and mozzarella cheese also goes very well with crisp corn chips.

Stuffed Crispy Potatoes

INGREDIENTS

Potatoes	8 medium sized	Cottage cheese *(paneer)* grated	3 tbsps
Capsicum	1 medium sized	Cheese (grated)	3 tbsps
Onion	1 medium sized	Oil	3 tbsps
Garlic	5-6 cloves	Dry herbs	½ tsp
Mushrooms	5-10	Pepper powder	¼ tsp
Carrot	1 medium sized	Salt	to taste

METHOD OF PREPARATION

1. Wash and dry the potatoes and prick deeply with a fork.

2. Wash, halve, de-seed and chop capsicum. Wash, peel and chop onion. Peel garlic and crush well. Wash and chop mushrooms. Wash, peel and grate carrot.

3. Place the potatoes on a paper towel and cook, uncovered, on Microwave HIGH (100%) for five minutes. Reposition and turn the potatoes over and continue cooking for five minutes until soft.

4. Remove the potatoes and cut in half, lengthwise and scoop out the pulp. Mash the pulp lightly with a fork.

5. Arrange the potato skins in a shallow microwave dish and pour a little of the oil around the insides. Brush some oil over the outside of the skins also. Cook, uncovered, on Microwave HIGH (100%) for eight minutes or until the skins are crispy.

6. Place capsicum, onion, garlic, mushrooms, carrot, grated *paneer* and dry herbs in a small microwave bowl and season to taste with salt, pepper and the remaining oil. Cover and cook on Microwave HIGH (100%) for five minutes until soft.

7. Mix the mashed potatoes with the vegetable mixture. Stuff the mixture into potato skins. Sprinkle the grated cheese on top.

8. Reheat, uncovered, on Microwave HIGH (100%) for three minutes. Alternatively grill TOP for three to five minutes. Serve immediately.

Pepper Prawns

INGREDIENTS

Prawns .... 10-12 small sized
Garlic .... 8-10 cloves
Tomato ketchup .... 2 tbsps
Salt .... to taste
Peppercorns (crushed) .... 2 tsps
Oil .... 1 tbsp

Vinegar .... 1 tbsp
Chilli sauce .... 1 tsp
Sugar .... 1 tsp
Cornstarch .... 1 tbsp
Dark soy sauce .... 1 tbsp

METHOD OF PREPARATION

1. Clean, remove heads and tails, de-vein and wash prawns thoroughly under running water. Drain and pat them dry. Peel and finely chop garlic.

2. Mix all the ingredients. Add two tablespoons of water and cook, uncovered on Microwave MEDIUM (70%) for three minutes.

3. Serve hot.

Smoky Fish Kabab

INGREDIENTS

Fish (pomfret/king fish) .... 1 (300-400 gms)

Stuffed olives 16

Baby onions 16

Tomatoes .... 2 medium sized

Oil .... 2 tbsps

Marinade

Lemon juice .... 3 tbsps

Peppercorns (crushed) .... 1 tsp

Salt .... to taste

Ginger paste .... 1 tbsp

Brown sugar .... 2 tbsps

METHOD OF PREPARATION

1. Clean and cut fish in fillets (boneless flat pieces). Wash fish fillets and cut into one-inch sized cubes.

2. Peel and wash baby onions. Wash, cut tomatoes into halves, de-seed and further cut into one-inch sized cubes.

3. Mix lemon juice, crushed pepper, salt, ginger paste and brown sugar. Marinate the fish, tomato and baby onions in this for an hour.

4. Skewer onto a toothpick or satay stick the marinated cubes in this order: fish cube, baby onion, stuffed olive and tomato cube. Arrange the toothpicks on a wire rack and cook on Grill TOP and BOTTOM for eight minutes.

5. Baste with oil and cook on Grill TOP and BOTTOM for four minutes. Serve immediately.

O Grill recipe

Stuffed Mushrooms

INGREDIENTS

Mushrooms .... 16 medium sized
Cottage cheese (crumbled) .... ¼ cup
Processed cheese (grated) .... ¼ cup
Onion .... 1 medium sized
Garlic .... 4-5 cloves
White pepper powder .... ¼ tsp
Nutmeg powder .... ¼ tsp
Salt .... to taste
Butter .... 5 tbsps
Lemon juice .... 1 tbsp

METHOD OF PREPARATION

1. Remove the stalks of mushrooms, clean well and chop finely. Keep aside.

2. Clean the heads of mushrooms and prepare them for stuffing.

3. Peel, wash and chop onion and garlic.

4. Take a microwave casserole and place chopped mushroom stalks, onion, garlic, cottage cheese, processed cheese, white pepper powder, nutmeg powder and salt in it. Mix well adding two tablespoons of butter.

5. Cook, uncovered, on Microwave HIGH (100%) for six minutes.

6. Stuff this mixture into the mushroom heads and sandwich two of such together, holding them with a toothpick.

7. Smear the remaining butter and lemon juice on mushrooms and cook, uncovered, on Microwave MEDIUM (70%) for three minutes. Serve hot.

CHEF'S TIP

Stuffed Mushrooms taste extra delicious with Pepper Chilli Sauce (ref. page 92). Vegetable stuffing can be substituted with chicken.

Kasuri Paneer Tikka

INGREDIENTS

Cottage cheese (*paneer*) .... 400 gms
Yogurt .... 1 cup
Gram flour (*besan*) .... 4 tbsps
Carom seeds (*ajwain*) .... ½ tsp
Garam masala powder .... 1 tsp
White pepper powder .... ½ tsp
Turmeric powder .... ½ tsp
Dried fenugreek leaves (*kasuri methi*) .....
.... 2 tsps

Ginger-garlic paste .... 1 tbsp
Green chilli paste .... 1 tbsp
Lemon juice .... 2 tbsps
Chaat masala .... ½ tsp
Butter .... 3 tbsps
Salt .... to taste
Oil .... 1 tbsp

METHOD OF PREPARATION

1. Cut cottage cheese into one and half inch sized squares of half a centimetre thickness.

2. Take a deep bowl and prepare a marinade by mixing together thickened yogurt, gram flour, carom seeds, *garam masala* powder, white pepper powder, turmeric powder, *kasuri methi*, ginger-garlic paste, green chilli paste, lemon juice, *chaat masala*, one tablespoon of melted butter and salt to taste.

3. Marinate *paneer* pieces in the mixture for half an hour.

4. Pre-heat the Convection oven at 230° C.

5. Place *paneer* pieces in a single layer on an ovenproof dish and baste them with oil.

6. Cook for twenty minutes at 230° C, basting with butter every five minutes and turning once after ten minutes.

7. Grill TOP for twelve minutes, basting with butter and turning once after six minutes.

8. Serve hot.

CHEF'S TIP
To thicken the yogurt, hang it tied in a muslin cloth and let it stand in the refrigerator for half an hour so that the excess water drains away.

○ Convection and Grill recipe

Vegetable Idli

INGREDIENTS

Parboiled rice *(ukda rice)* .... 1 cup
Black gram split *(urad dal)* .... ½ cup
Salt .... to taste
Fresh Coriander leaves .... a few sprigs
Carrot .... 1 medium sized
French beans 4-5
Cauliflower .... 2-3 florets
Capsicum .... ½ medium sized
Oil .... 2 tbsps
Peppercorns (crushed) .... 1 tbsp

METHOD OF PREPARATION

1. Wash and soak the rice and *urad dal* separately for at least four hours. Drain and grind rice to a coarse and *dal* to a fine batter using enough water.

2. Mix both the batters adding sufficient water to get a dropping consistency.

3. Add salt and allow it to ferment for six to eight hours or overnight covered in a warm place.

4. Wash and chop coriander leaves. Peel, wash and grate carrot. String, wash and chop French beans. Wash and grate the cauliflower florets. Wash, de-seed and chop capsicum.

5. Add the vegetables to the fermented batter. Mix well.

6. Lightly grease the *idli* stand with oil. Pour a spoonful of batter into each dent. Garnish with crushed peppercorns and chopped coriander leaves.

7. Keep a cupful of water along with the *idli* stand in the microwave oven, cover and cook on Microwave HIGH (100%) for four minutes. Allow standing time of five minutes before serving.

CHEF'S TIP

If you do not have a microwave *idli* stand, you can use small glass bowls (*katori* sized) to make *idlis*.

Four Seasons Pizza

INGREDIENTS

Pizza base .... 2 (9 inches in diameter)

For the sauce

Tomatoes .... 2 medium sized
Onion .... ½ small sized
Garlic .... 2 cloves
Basil leaves 2
Oregano .... a pinch
Pepper powder .... a pinch
Olive oil .... 1 tbsp
Tomato puree .... ½ cup
Salt .... to taste

For the topping

Capsicums .... 2 medium sized
Tomatoes .... 2 medium sized
Cottage cheese (*paneer*) .... 200 gms
Mushrooms 10-12
Stuffed green olives 4-5
Stuffed black olives 4-5
Corn kernels .... ½ cup
Mozzarella cheese (grated) .... 2 cups
Red chilli flakes .... 2 tsps
Dry oregano .... ½ tsp

METHOD OF PREPARATION

For the sauce

1. Wash and quarter the tomatoes. Peel, wash and chop onion. Peel and chop garlic. Wash and tear basil leaves with hands.

2. Place tomatoes in a microwave bowl and cook, uncovered, on Microwave HIGH (100%) or three minutes.

3. Mix in rest of the ingredients and cook, uncovered, on Microwave HIGH (100%) for three minutes.

4. Let cool and blend into a smooth sauce.

For the topping

5. Wash, remove the top and de-seed the capsicum. Cut into half a centimetre thick round slices.

6. Wash and cut the tomato into half a centimetre thick round slices. Cut the *paneer* into half a centimetre thick triangular slices with each side being one inch.

7. Wash and thinly slice the mushrooms. Thinly slice green and black olives.

For the pizza

8. Spread the sauce on each pizza base. Spread half the grated cheese equally on both. Arrange corn on one quarter of each pizza, mushroom slices on the second quarter, capsicum and tomato slices on the third quarter, *paneer* slices on the fourth quarter. Sprinkle red chilli flakes, oregano and the remaining cheese. Spread the green olive slices over the *paneer* slices and black olive slices over the mushroom slices. Place on a microwave plate and cook, uncovered, on Microwave LOW (40%) or two minutes or alternatively, cook in the Grill TOP for ten minutes.

> **CHEF'S TIP**
> The pizza bases can be baked in advance and finishing can be done with the sauce and the topping.

O Microwave and Grill recipe

Three Flavour Popcorn

INGREDIENTS

Sweet

Dried corn kernels .... ½ cup   Oil ....1 tbsp
Brown sugar .... ¾ cup

METHOD OF PREPARATION

Mix oil, brown sugar and corn in a microwave bowl. Cover and cook on Microwave HIGH (100%) for six minutes, stirring once after three minutes.

INGREDIENTS

Savoury

Dried corn kernels .... ½ cup   Cheese powder .... 2 tbsps
Oil .... 1 tbsp   Red chilli flakes .... 1½ tbsps

METHOD OF PREPARATION

Mix oil and corn in a microwave bowl. Cover and cook on Microwave HIGH (100%) for six minutes, stirring once after three minutes. Add cheese powder and red chilli flakes and toss.

INGREDIENTS

Savoury

Dried corn kernels .... ½ cup   Tomato powder ....1 tbsp
Oil .... 1 tbsp   Salt.. to taste

METHOD OF PREPARATION

Mix oil and corn in a microwave bowl. Cover and cook on Microwave HIGH (100%) for six minutes, stirring once after three minutes. Add tomato powder and salt to taste and toss.

CHEF'S TIP

Try out an interesting combination of all the popcorns namely caramel, chilli cheese and tomato. It happened to me once accidentally!

Kaanda Poha

INGREDIENTS

Thick *poha* .... 2 cups	Curry leaves 8-10
Onions .... 3 medium sized	Turmeric powder .... 1 tsp
Green chillies 3-4	Salt .... to taste
Roasted peanuts (optional) .... ¼ cup	Lemon juice .... 1 tbsp
Oil .... 2 tbsps	Fresh coriander leaves .... a few sprigs

METHOD OF PREPARATION

1. Wash *poha* thoroughly. Keep in a strainer so that the excess water gets drained out.

2. Peel, wash and finely chop onions. Remove stems, wash, de-seed and slit green chillies into two. Clean, wash and chop coriander leaves finely.

3. Take oil and onions in a microwave bowl. Add slit green chillies, curry leaves, roasted peanuts and cook, uncovered, on Microwave HIGH (100%) for three minutes.

4. Add turmeric powder, *poha* and salt. Mix well and cook, covered, on Microwave HIGH (100%) for five minutes.

5. Add lemon juice. Mix well, garnish with chopped coriander leaves and serve hot.

Chicken Flower Dumplings

INGREDIENTS

Chicken mince	1 cup	Ginger paste	1 tsp
Long grain rice	¼ cup	Salt	to taste
Green chillies	3-4	Peppercorns	4-5

METHOD OF PREPARATION

1. Wash rice twice and soak in half a cup of water for an hour. Drain off excess water.

2. Remove stems, wash green chillies and chop. Crush peppercorns.

3. Mix chicken mince with chillies, ginger paste, salt and freshly crushed peppercorns. Divide this mixture into twelve equal portions.

4. Form round balls from each portion of chicken mix and then roll them in presoaked rice.

5. In a large microwave casserole, pour in eight cups of water. Cover and place on Microwave HIGH (100%) for twelve to fifteen minutes or till it starts to boil. Gently add the chicken balls and cook, covered, on microwave HIGH (100%) for eight minutes.

6. Drain and serve hot with a dip of your choice.

CHEF'S TIP

To get the best result you should use chicken mince that is extra fine, preferably made from chicken breast only.

Tangdi Kabab

INGREDIENTS

Chicken drumsticks 8
(chicken legs without thigh section) ....
Lemon juice .... 1 tbsp
Ginger .... 1 inch
Garlic .... 6 cloves
Green chillies 4-6
Skimmed milk yogurt .... 1 cup
Gram flour *(besan)* .... 2 tbsps

Turmeric powder .... ½ tsp
Garam masala powder .... 1 tsp
Red chilli powder .... 1 tsp
Salt .... to taste
Chaat masala powder .... 2 tsps
Lemon wedges .... for garnishing
Oil .... 3 tbsps

METHOD OF PREPARATION

1. Clean and trim excess fat and skin from the drumsticks. Dry them with a clean and absorbent kitchen towel. Make three to four long deep incisions. Apply lemon juice and keep aside.

2. Peel ginger and garlic, wash and grind them to a paste.

3. Wash green chillies, remove stems and then chop them fine.

4. Hang skimmed milk yogurt for fifteen to twenty minutes to drain off excess water.

5. Roast gram flour in a microwave bowl on Microwave LOW (50%) for five minutes stirring twice in between. Cool and mix with hung yogurt, ginger and garlic paste, turmeric powder, *garam masala* powder, red chilli powder, salt and chopped green chillies.

6. Marinate chicken drumsticks in the above mixture and refrigerate for one to two hours.

7. Preheat Convection oven to 220°C.

8. Place marinated chicken drumsticks on a flat dish and roast for five minutes in the preheated oven. Reduce oven temperature to 180°C and further cook for fifteen to twenty minutes or till completely cooked. Turn and baste drumsticks with oil a couple of times to ensure even cooking and colour.

9. Serve hot sprinkled with *chaat masala* and lemon wedges.

O Convection recipe

Kheema Tikki Kabab

INGREDIENTS

Lamb mince *(kheema)* .... 400 gms
Mutton fat .... 100 gms
Onions .... 2 medium sized
Green chillies 3-4
Fresh coriander leaves .... 4 sprigs
Garlic paste .... 1 tbsp
Ginger paste .... 1 tbsp

Cumin powder .... 1 tsp
Garam masala powder .... 1 tsp
Kashmiri red chilli powder .... 2 tsps
Salt .... to taste
Oil for basting .... ½ cup
Chaat masala .... 2 tsps
Lemon juice .... 2 tsps

METHOD OF PREPARATION

1. Peel, wash and chop onions. Remove stems, wash and chop green chillies. Wash and chop coriander leaves.

2. Place lamb mince, mutton fat, onions, green chillies and coriander leaves in a mixer and grind twice so that it is a smooth mixture.

3. Mix in garlic paste, ginger paste, cumin powder, *garam masala* powder, Kashmiri red chilli powder and salt to taste.

4. Divide mince mixture into sixteen equal portions.

5. Shape into flat round shapes of one inch diameter and one centimetre thickness and place them on a roasting tray.

6. Grill TOP and BOTTOM for fifteen to twenty minutes turning them over once.

7. While cooking, brush with oil every five minutes to get an even brown crust.

8. Serve hot, sprinkled with *chaat masala* and lemon juice.

CHEF'S TIP

Papaya or pineapple paste can be added to the mutton mince to get succulent and tender *kababs*.

O Grill recipe

Murgh Makhmali Kabab

INGREDIENTS

Chicken breasts .... 4 (800 gms)	Nutmeg powder .... ½ tsp
Green chillies 4-6	*Garam masala* powder .... 2 tsps
Ginger .... 1 inch piece	Honey .... 1 tbsp
Garlic .... 5-6 cloves	Lemon juice .... ½ tbsp
Yogurt .... ⅔ cup	Salt .... to taste
Processed cheese (grated) .... ¼ cup	Butter .... ¼ cup
Fresh cream .... ¼ cup	

METHOD OF PREPARATION

1. Clean, skin, de-bone and cut each breast into two. Remove stems and wash green chillies, wash and peel ginger and peel garlic cloves. Grind green chillies, ginger and garlic into a smooth paste. Rub it well onto chicken pieces. Cover and keep aside for fifteen minutes.

2. Hang yogurt in a muslin cloth for half an hour and drain away the whey.

3. Mix thickened yogurt, cheese, cream, nutmeg powder, *garam masala* powder, honey, lemon juice and salt to taste. Whisk the ingredients well and marinate the chicken pieces in this mixture for three hours in a refrigerator.

4. Place chicken pieces, an inch apart, on a wire rack.

5. Cook chicken in Grill TOP and BOTTOM for twenty minutes, brushing with butter every five minutes. Serve hot with *chutney* of your choice.

CHEF'S TIP

Use chicken supreme if possible for they make the *kababs* succulent and tender.

○ Grill recipe

Shrimps
in Garlic Butter

INGREDIENTS

Shrimps	400 gms	Mustard paste	1 tbsp
Parsley	a few sprigs	Lemon juice	1 tbsp
Butter	4 tbsps	Peppercorns	8-10
Garlic paste	3 tbsps	Salt	to taste

METHOD OF PREPARATION

1. Remove heads and shells of shrimps. De-vein and wash well. Drain thoroughly.

2. Wash and dry parsley. Chop finely and keep aside. Crush the peppercorns.

3. Place shrimps, butter, garlic paste, parsley, mustard paste, lemon juice and freshly crushed peppercorns in a microwave bowl. Mix well adding salt to taste.

4. Cook, uncovered, on Microwave HIGH (100%) for three minutes. Serve hot, preferably with toothpicks.

Corn Crusted Chicken

INGREDIENTS

Chicken (boneless) .... ½ kg	Oil .... 3 tbsps
Oil .... 2 tbsps	Red chilli powder .... 2 tbsps
For the marinade	Salt .... to taste
Mustard powder .... 1 tsp	**Coating**
Green chillies 2-3	Eggs 2
Garlic paste .... 2 tbsps	Salt .... to taste
Lemon juice .... 2 tbsps	Cornflakes .... ½ cup
Garam masala powder .... 2 tsps	

METHOD OF PREPARATION

1. Wash chicken and cut into one and half inch sized cubes.

2. Remove stems, wash and chop green chillies.

3. Combine chicken with marinade ingredients and set aside for an hour in a refrigerator.

4. Beat egg and add salt to it.

5. Lightly crush the cornflakes using a rolling pin.

6. Roll the chicken cubes in egg and coat with crushed cornflakes pressing them firmly onto the chicken cubes.

7. Preheat Convection oven to 200°C.

8. Place chicken on the wire rack. Cook in the preheated oven at 200°C for fifteen to twenty minutes or till the chicken pieces are fully cooked.

> **NOTE**
> You can serve the chicken with Sichuan Sauce or Tomato Ketchup.
> Refer page no.127 for the recipe of Sichuan Sauce

O Convection recipe

Celery Corn Medley

INGREDIENTS

Sweetcorn kernels	1 cup	Peppercorns	5-6
Celery stalks	2	Oil	2 tsps
Tomatoes	4 medium sized	Brown sugar	1 tbsp
Onion	1 medium sized	Tomato ketchup	2 tbsps
Garlic	4-5 cloves	Salt	to taste
Capsicum	1 medium sized	Fresh parsley	few sprigs
Fresh mushrooms	8-10		

METHOD OF PREPARATION

1. Wash and slice celery stalk into one-inch sized pieces. Wash and cut tomatoes into quarters. Peel, wash and chop onion. Peel and crush garlic. Wash, halve, de-seed capsicum and dice. Remove stem, clean, wash and slice mushrooms. Crush peppercorns.

2. Put tomatoes into a large microwave bowl with onion and garlic. Cover and cook on Microwave HIGH (100%) for five minutes, until a thick and pulpy sauce results, stirring twice in between.

3. Combine the celery, capsicum, corn kernels and oil in a medium sized microwave bowl. Cover and cook on Microwave HIGH (100%) for three minutes, or until the vegetables are just tender. Remove and stir.

4. Mix brown sugar, tomato ketchup, salt, peppercorns, celery, capsicum, mushrooms and corn into the tomato sauce. Cover and cook on Microwave HIGH (100%) for three minutes, stirring once. Sprinkle with chopped parsley and serve hot.

Stir-fried Vegetables

INGREDIENTS

Cauliflower	¼ medium sized	Oil	2 tbsps
French beans	8	Salt	to taste
Carrot	1 medium sized	White pepper powder	½ tsp
Capsicums	2 medium sized	Ajinomoto (optional)	¼ tsp
Babycorn	6	Soy sauce	1 tsp
Mushrooms	4-5	Sugar	¼ tsp
Spring onions	2-3	Cornstarch	2 tsps

METHOD OF PREPARATION

1. Wash cauliflower and separate into one inch sized florets. String, wash and cut French beans into diamond shaped pieces each side measuring half inch. Peel, wash and cut carrot into thin slices.

2. Wash, halve, de-seed and cut capsicums into thick strips. Wash babycorn and slice into roundels. Clean, wash and cut mushrooms into thick slices. Take bulbs of spring onions, peel, wash and cut into quarters. Wash and chop two spring onion greens for garnish. Dissolve cornstarch in quarter cup of water.

3. Place cauliflower, French beans, carrot and babycorn in a microwave casserole, add one cup of water. Cook, uncovered, on Microwave HIGH (100%) for five minutes. Drain well.

4. Take oil in a microwave bowl. Add cauliflower, French beans, carrot, capsicum, babycorn, onions and mushrooms. Cook, uncovered, on microwave HIGH (100%) for two minutes. Add salt, white pepper powder, ajinomoto, soy sauce and sugar.

5. Add dissolved cornstarch mixture to the vegetables. Stir well and cook, uncovered, for two minutes on Microwave HIGH (100%). Remove and serve immediately.

Cauliflower & Broccoli in Spiced Almond Sauce

INGREDIENTS

Cauliflower .... ½ small sized
Broccoli .... ½ small sized
Onion............................ 1 medium sized
Garlic ,,,,,,,,,,, ... 5-6 cloves
Capsicum ,,,,,,,,,, ... 1 medium sized
Peppercorns ,,,,,,,,,, ... 5-6
Almonds 10-12
Butter .... 3 tbsps

Red chilli flakes .... 1 tsp
Tomato puree .... ¼ cup
Tomato ketchup .... 2 tbsps
Salt .... to taste
Nutmeg powder .... ¼ tsp
White sauce* .... ½ cup
Dried mixed herbs .... ¼ tsp

METHOD OF PREPARATION

1. Wash and cut cauliflower and broccoli into one inch sized florets. Peel, wash and chop onion and garlic. Wash, halve, de-seed and cut capsicum into half inch sized cubes. Crush peppercorns. Blanch almonds in one cup of water on Microwave HIGH (100%) uncovered for two minutes. Drain, peel and grind it to a fine paste with half a cup of water.

2. Mix butter, onion, garlic in a deep microwave bowl and cook on Microwave HIGH (100%) for two minutes.

3. Add cauliflower, capsicum, red chilli flakes and cook, covered, on Microwave HIGH (100%) for three minutes.

4. Add tomato puree, tomato ketchup, salt, crushed peppercorns, nutmeg powder, white sauce, mixed herbs, almond paste, broccoli and half a cup of water. Stir and cook, covered, on Microwave HIGH (100%) for six minutes.

> **NOTE**
> *Refer page no. 126 for the recipe of White Sauce.

Spicy Bhindi

INGREDIENTS

Lady fingers (*bhindi*) .... ½ kg
Green chillies 3–4
Ginger..................................... 1 inch piece
Onion............................. 1 medium sized
Fennel seeds (*saunf*) ....1 tsp
Fenugreek seeds .... ¼ tsp

Oil .... 2 tsps
Cumin seeds .... 1 tsp
Coriander powder ....1 tbsp
Dry mango powder (*amchur*) .... 1 tsp
Red chilli powder .... 2 tsps
Salt.. to taste

METHOD OF PREPARATION

1. Wash, wipe and cut head and tail of lady fingers. Cut each into two or three pieces depending on the size. Remove stems, wash and finely chop green chillies. Peel, wash and finely chop ginger. Peel, wash and slice onion thinly. Crush fennel seeds and fenugreek seeds lightly.

2. Place oil, crushed fennel seeds, fenugreek seeds, cumin seeds, onion, green chillies, ginger, coriander powder in a deep microwave casserole. Mix well. Cook on Microwave HIGH (100%) for two minutes.

3. Mix in the lady fingers, dry mango powder, red chilli powder and salt. Cook, covered, on Microwave HIGH (100%) for six minutes.

4. Stir and cook further, uncovered, on Microwave HIGH (100%) for one minute. Serve immediately.

Badami Babycorn Paneer Masala

INGREDIENTS

Babycorn 10-12	Tomato puree .... 2 cups
Cottage cheese *(paneer)* .... 200 gms	Salt .... to taste
Onions .... 2 medium sized	Red chilli powder .... 1 tsp
Garlic .... 4-5 cloves	Cumin powder .... ½ tsp
Ginger .... 2 inch piece	Coriander powder .... 2 tsps
Red chillies whole 3-4	*Garam masala* powder .... 1 tsp
Almonds 12-15	Dry fenugreek leaves *(kasuri methi)* ....
Oil .... 3 tbsps	.... 1 tbsp

METHOD OF PREPARATION

1. Wash and thinly slice the babycorn. Cut *paneer* into one inch sized triangular pieces. Peel, wash and roughly chop onions and garlic. Peel, wash and chop half the ginger and cut the remaining half into julienne for garnish.

2. Remove stems of whole red chillies. Grind the red chillies, almonds, onions, garlic and ginger into a fine paste using half a cup of water.

3. Take oil alongwith ground paste, tomato puree, salt and half a cup of water in a microwave bowl. Cook, covered on Microwave HIGH (100%) for four minutes.

4. Stir and add sliced babycorn, *paneer* pieces, red chilli powder, cumin powder, coriander powder and *garam masala* powder and mix well. Cover and cook on Microwave HIGH (100%) for ten minutes.

5. Take the *kasuri methi* in a microwave plate and roast, uncovered, on Microwave HIGH (100 %) for half a minute. Remove, crush and sprinkle over the gravy. Serve hot.

Aloo Anardana

INGREDIENTS

Baby potatoes 25-30	Coriander powder .... 1 tbsp
Oil .... 2 tbsps	Cumin powder .... ½ tsp
Dried pomegranate seeds *(anardana)*	Red chilli powder .... 1 tsp
.... 2 tbsps	Salt .... to taste
Green chillies 3-4	Fresh pomegranate seeds .... ¼ cup
Fresh coriander leaves .... 4-5 sprigs	*Chaat masala* .... 1 tbsp
Turmeric powder .... ½ tsp	

METHOD OF PREPARATION

1. Wash potatoes and wipe them dry.

2. Smear one tablespoon oil on the potatoes and place them in a microwave plate and cook on Microwave MEDIUM (70%) for ten minutes.

3. Crush dry *anardana*. Remove stems, wash and chop green chillies. Wash, dry and chop coriander leaves.

4. Place remaining oil in a microwave casserole. Add turmeric powder, coriander powder, cumin powder, red chilli powder, crushed *anardana*, green chillies, salt and the cooked potatoes. Mix well. Cook, uncovered, on Microwave HIGH (100%) for five minutes.

5. Turn the potatoes once and cook further on Microwave MEDIUM (70%) for five minutes.

6. Remove, stir in fresh pomegranate seeds, sprinkle with chopped coriander leaves and *chaat masala* and serve hot.

Dahi Baingan

INGREDIENTS

Long brinjals .... 3-4 medium sized
Yogurt .... 1 cup
Ginger-garlic paste .... 2 tsps
Coriander powder .... 2 tsps
Garam masala powder .... 1 tsp
Red chilli powder .... 1 tsp
Cumin powder .... ½ tsp
Turmeric powder .... 1 tsp
Salt .... to taste

Onions .... 2 medium sized
Green chillies 3-4
Fresh coriander leaves .... 5-6 sprigs
Gram flour (*besan*) .... ½ cup
Oil .... 5 tbsps
Red chillies whole 3
Cumin seeds .... 1 tsp
Asafoetida .... ¼ tsp

METHOD OF PREPARATION

1. Wash brinjals, de-stem and cut into one inch sized cubes. Add ginger-garlic paste, coriander powder, *garam masala* powder, red chilli powder, cumin powder, turmeric powder, salt to taste and mix well. Cover and keep aside to marinate for five minutes.

2. Peel, wash and chop onions. Wash, remove stems and chop green chillies. Wash and chop coriander leaves.

3. Beat together yogurt and gram flour. Mix in four cups of water. Keep aside.

4. In a deep microwave bowl put in two tablespoons of oil with onions and mix well. Add green chillies and marinated brinjal cubes. Cook, uncovered, on Microwave HIGH (100%) for fifteen minutes, stirring once or twice in between. Stir in yogurt mixture.

5. Cook, uncovered, on Microwave HIGH (100%) for ten minutes.

6. In a medium sized microwave casserole place the remaining oil, whole red chillies broken into two, cumin seeds and asafoetida. Cook, uncovered, on Microwave HIGH (100%) for four minutes. Remove and mix immediately into the cooked brinjal. Serve hot, garnished with chopped coriander leaves.

> **CHEF'S TIP**
> Select the brinjals carefully. Those which are light in weight give the best results.

Paneer Makhani

INGREDIENTS

Cottage cheese *(paneer)* .... 400 gms	Garlic paste .... 1 tbsp
Green chillies 2-3	Tomato puree .... 2 cups
Butter .... ¼ cup	Kashmiri red chilli powder .... 1 tbsp
Bay leaves 2	*Garam masala* powder .... 1 tsp
Peppercorns 8-10	Salt .... to taste
Cinnamon .... 2 inch stick	Sugar/honey .... 2 tbsps
Green cardamoms 5	Dried fenugreek leaves
Cloves 10	*(kasuri methi)* .... ½ tsp
Ginger paste .... 1 tbsp	Fresh cream .... 1 cup

METHOD OF PREPARATION

1. Cut the *paneer* into one inch sized cubes or triangles. Remove stems, wash and chop green chillies.

2. Take butter in a microwave dish, heat uncovered, for thirty seconds on Microwave HIGH (100%). Add bay leaves, peppercorns, cinnamon, green cardamoms and cloves. Add ginger paste, garlic paste and green chillies. Stir well and cook, uncovered, on Microwave HIGH (100%) for three minutes.

3. Add tomato puree, Kashmiri red chilli powder, *garam masala* powder, salt and one and a half cups of water. Cook, covered, on Microwave HIGH (100%) for ten minutes.

4. Add sugar or honey and crushed *kasuri methi*. Adjust salt and mix well.

5. Add the *paneer* pieces, cook, uncovered on Microwave MEDIUM (70%) for eight minutes.

6. Add fresh cream. Cook, uncovered, on Microwave LOW (50%) for two to three minutes. Serve hot.

Mirchi ka Salan

INGREDIENTS

Green chillies .... 20 big sized
Oil .... 4 tbsps
Onion .... 1 medium sized
Ginger .... 1 inch piece
Garlic .... 6-8 cloves
Sesame seeds .... 2 tbsps
Coriander seeds .... 1 tbsp
Cumin seeds .... 1 tsp

Roasted peanuts .... ½ cup
Red chillies whole 2
Mustard seeds .... 1 tsp
Curry leaves 8-10
Turmeric powder .... ½ tsp
Tamarind pulp .... 4 tbsps
Salt .... to taste

METHOD OF PREPARATION

1. Wash, wipe and slit green chillies lengthwise. Place in a microwave casserole with one tablespoon of oil and cook, uncovered, on Microwave HIGH (100%) for four minutes. Place them on a paper towel and keep aside.

2. Peel, wash and grate onion. Wash, peel ginger and chop roughly. Peel garlic.

3. Place a mixture of sesame seeds, coriander seeds and cumin seeds in microwave plate. Roast, uncovered, on Microwave HIGH (100%) for four minutes.

4. Grind roasted peanuts, sesame seeds, coriander seeds, cumin seeds, whole red chillies, ginger and garlic into a smooth paste, using a little water if necessary.

5. Take remaining oil in a microwave dish, add mustard seeds, curry leaves and onion. Cook, uncovered, on Microwave MEDIUM (80%) for six minutes until lightly browned.

6. Add turmeric powder and mix well. Add *masala* paste. Put one and a half cups of water and cook, uncovered, on Microwave HIGH (100%) for eight minutes.

7. Dissolve tamarind pulp in half a cup of water and add it to the casserole.

8. Add green chillies and salt and mix well. Cook, uncovered, on Microwave LOW (60%) for four minutes.

9. Serve hot.

NOTE

In Hyderabad, traditionally Mirchi ka Salan is served with *biryanis*. This gravy is referred to as *Tili* (*Til* – Sesame) *aur Falli* (*Moongfalli* – Peanuts) gravy.

CHEF'S TIP

Use large sized chillies for not only will they retain shape after being cooked but also because they are not very hot.

Stuffed Capsicums

INGREDIENTS

Capsicums .... 12 medium sized
Green chillies 3-4
Onion .... 1 medium sized
Ginger .... 1 inch piece
Fresh coriander leaves .... a few sprigs
Cottage cheese *(paneer)* .... 100 gms
Cashewnuts 8-10
Raisins *(kishmish)* 12-15

Potatoes .... 3 medium sized
Dry mango powder *(amchur)* ...... 2 tsps
Red chilli powder .... 1½ tsps
Cumin powder .... 1 tsp
Garam masala powder .... 1 tsp
Salt .... to taste
Oil .... 2 tbsps
Cheese *(grated)* .... ½ cup

METHOD OF PREPARATION

1. Wash capsicums, slice off thinly from the top and remove the seeds to make it hollow. Similarly slice off thinly from the bottom so that the capsicums stand steady when placed on the baking tray.

2. Remove stems, wash and chop the green chillies. Peel, wash and chop onion and ginger. Clean, wash and finely chop coriander leaves. Grate *paneer*. Grind cashewnuts coarsely. Wash the raisins and wipe them dry.

3. Wash, wipe dry and place the potatoes in a microwave dish and cook, covered, on Microwave HIGH (100%) for six to seven minutes. Allow to cool slightly before peeling and mashing them.

4. Mix mashed potatoes, *paneer*, cashewnuts, raisins, *amchur*, red chilli powder, cumin powder, *garam masala* powder, coriander leaves and salt well. Keep aside.

5. Take oil, ginger, onion and green chillies in a microwave bowl, cover and cook on Microwave HIGH (100%) for two minutes.

6. Add potato mixture and cook again, covered, on Microwave HIGH (100%) for two minutes. Stir well.

7. Divide this mixture evenly into twelve portions and stuff into the prepared capsicum shells, sprinkle cheese and place on a microwave plate. Cook, uncovered, on Microwave HIGH (90%) for four minutes.

8. Serve hot.

Coconut Peas

INGREDIENTS

Peas (shelled)	1½ cups	Cumin seeds	½ tsp
Salt	to taste	Asafoetida	¼ tsp
Onion	1 medium sized	Curry leaves	5-6
Ginger	½ inch piece	**For garnish**	
Green chillies	3	Lemon juice	3 tsps
Oil	2 tsps	Coconut (freshly scraped)	¼ cup
Mustard seeds	½ tsp		

METHOD OF PREPARATION

1. Place peas in a microwave casserole with three cups of water and salt to taste. Cook, uncovered, on Microwave HIGH (100%) for five minutes. Remove, drain, refresh in cold water and keep aside.

2. Peel, wash and chop onion and ginger. Remove stems, wash and slit green chillies.

3. In a microwave casserole mix onion, green chillies, ginger, oil, mustard seeds, cumin seeds, asafoetida and curry leaves. Cook, uncovered, on Microwave HIGH (100%) for three minutes.

4. Add cooked peas and salt. Cook further, covered, on Microwave HIGH (100%) for three minutes. Add lemon juice and scraped fresh coconut and mix well. Serve immediately.

Aloo Palak Bhaji

INGREDIENTS

Potatoes .... 4 medium sized	Cumin seeds .... 1 tsp
Spinach .... 1 medium sized bunch	Coriander powder .... 2 tsps
Onion............................ 1 medium sized	Lemon juice .... ½ tsp
Oil... 2 tbsps	Salt.. to taste
Garlic .... 6-8 cloves	*Garam masala* powder .... ½ tsp
Green chillies 3-4	

METHOD OF PREPARATION

1. Peel, wash and cut potatoes into half-inch sized cubes. Clean and wash spinach under running water. Drain and shred. Peel and finely chop onion and garlic. Remove stems, wash and finely chop green chillies.

2. Take a large microwave casserole and place oil, cumin seeds, chopped onion and garlic. Cook, uncovered, on Microwave HIGH (100%) for two minutes.

3. Add potatoes with half cup of water and stir well. Cover and cook on Microwave HIGH (100%) for six minutes..

4. Add spinach and green chillies and cook further on Microwave HIGH (100%) for six minutes.

5. Stir in lemon juice, salt and *garam masala* powder to taste. Serve hot.

Vegetables in Chilli Mustard Sauce

INGREDIENTS

Green peas (shelled) .... ½ cup	Green chillies 3
French beans 5-6	Spring onion bulbs 2
Cauliflower .... ½ small sized	Mustard paste .... 1 tbsp
Capsicum .... 1 medium sized	Red chilli sauce .... 3 tbsps
Carrot .... 1 medium sized	Fresh cream ...., ½ cup
Mushrooms 5-6	Salt.. to taste
Oil .... 2 tbsps	Pepper powder .... ¼ tsp

METHOD OF PREPARATION

1. Place peas with one cup of water in a microwave bowl. Cook, uncovered, at Microwave HIGH (100%) for five minutes. Drain and refresh in cold water.

2. String, wash and cut French beans into diamonds each side measuring half inch. Wash and separate cauliflower into small florets. Wash, de-seed and cut capsicum into half inch sized dices. Peel, wash and slice carrot diagonally into half centimetre thick pieces. Clean, wash and slice mushrooms thickly. Remove stems, wash and finely chop green chillies. Peel, wash and finely chop spring onions.

3. Place cauliflower, French beans and carrot in a microwave bowl with one cup of water and cook, covered, on Microwave HIGH (100%) for eight minutes. Drain and keep aside.

4. In a deep microwave casserole, mix oil, green chillies, spring onions, capsicum and cook uncovered on Microwave HIGH (100%) for two minutes.

5. Add peas, cauliflower, French beans, carrot, mushrooms, mustard paste, chilli sauce and fresh cream. Season with salt and pepper and cook, covered, on Microwave HIGH (100%) for two minutes. Serve hot.

Reshmi Kofta Curry

INGREDIENTS

For koftas

Potatoes .... 3 large sized	
Cottage cheese *(paneer)*(grated) ..... ½ cup	
Green chillies 2-3	
Raisins *(kishmish)* 10-12	
Cornstarch .... 2 tbsps	
Salt .... to taste	
Oil .... 4-5 tbsps	

For gravy

Onions .... 2 medium sized
Green chillies 2-3
Poppy seeds *(khus khus)* .... 3 tbsps

Yogurt .... ½ cup
Oil .... 2 tbsps
Ginger paste .... 1 tbsp
Garlic paste .... 1 tbsp
Sugar .... ½ tsp
Red chilli powder .... 1½ tsps
Garam masala powder .... 2 tsps
Salt .... to taste
Fresh cream .... ¾ cup

For garnish
Fresh coriander leaves .... a few sprigs

METHOD OF PREPARATION

For koftas

1. Wash potatoes and cut each into two. Place in a microwave bowl and sprinkle two tablespoons of water. Cover and cook on Microwave HIGH (100%) for six minutes. Let it cool.

2. Remove stems, wash and finely chop green chillies. Wash raisins and pat them dry.

3. Peel and mash potatoes and mix in grated *paneer*, raisins, green chillies, cornstarch and salt to taste. Divide into ten to twelve portions and roll them into cylindrical shapes. Sprinkle each croquette with oil and cook on Grill TOP and BOTTOM for fifteen minutes. Keep aside.

For gravy

4. Peel, wash and cut onions into quarters. Place in a small microwave casserole with half a cup of water and cook, covered, on Microwave HIGH (100%) for five minutes. Cool and grind to a smooth paste. Remove stems, wash and finely chop green chillies.

5. Soak poppy seeds in a quarter cup of water for fifteen-twenty minutes. Grind to a fine paste. Whisk yogurt with a quarter cup of water.

6. In a deep microwave casserole mix oil, onions, ginger and garlic pastes, green chillies and cook, uncovered, on Microwave HIGH (100%) for three minutes.

7. Stir in yogurt, poppy seed paste, sugar, red chilli powder, *garam masala* powder and salt to taste. Cover and cook on Microwave HIGH (100%) for three minutes. Stir in fresh cream. Cook further, uncovered, on Microwave HIGH (100%) for a minute.

To serve

8. Wash, dry and finely chop coriander leaves.

9. Arrange *koftas* in a serving dish, pour gravy and serve hot, sprinkled with chopped coriander leaves.

O Microwave and Grill recipe

Sweet & Sour Vegetables

INGREDIENTS

Mushrooms 6	Ginger paste .... ½ tsp
Green capsicums .... 2 medium sized	Garlic paste (optional) .... ½ tsp
French beans 8-10	Pepper powder .... ½ tsp
Cauliflower .... ½ medium sized	Ajinomoto .... a pinch
Onions .... 2 medium sized	Salt .... to taste
Carrots .... 2 medium sized	Vegetable stock* or water .... 1 cup
For sauce	Tomato ketchup .... ¾ cup
Cornstarch .... 3¼ tbsps	Soy sauce .... 1½ tbsps
Spring onions 2	Sugar .... 3 tbsps
Oil .... 2 tbsps	Vinegar .... 1/3 cup

METHOD OF PREPARATION

1. Clean and cut mushrooms into thick slices. Wash, halve, de-seed and cut capsicums into two centimetre sized dices. String, wash French beans and cut into two centimetre sized pieces. Separate cauliflower into one inch sized florets and wash well. Peel, wash and cut onions and carrots into two centimetre sized dices.

2. Peel and wash spring onions and slice thinly. Wash three-four spring onion greens and chop finely. Keep aside for garnish.

3. Place French beans, cauliflower and carrots in a microwave bowl with one cup of water. Cover and cook on Microwave HIGH (100%) for six minutes.

4. In another bowl mix cornstarch with a quarter cup of water.

5. Place oil, ginger paste, garlic paste, spring onions, pepper powder, ajinomoto and salt in a deep microwave casserole. Mix well and cook, uncovered, on Microwave HIGH (100%) for two minutes.

6. Add vegetable stock, tomato ketchup, soy sauce, sugar and vinegar and mix well.

7. Cook, covered, on Microwave HIGH (100%) for six minutes. Add French beans, cauliflower, capsicum, mushrooms, carrots and onions and mix well.

8. Cook, covered, on Microwave HIGH (100%) for five minutes. Stir in cornstarch mixture. Cook further, uncovered, on Microwave HIGH (100%) for eight minutes.

9. Garnish with spring onion greens and serve immediately.

NOTE
*Refer page no. 124 for the recipe of Vegetable Stock.

Prawn Balchao

INGREDIENTS

Prawns/shrimps (shelled) .... 500 gms	Mustard seeds .... 1 tsp
Ginger .... 2 inch piece	Malt vinegar .... 1 cup
Garlic ....15-20 cloves	Onions........................... 2 medium sized
Cumin seeds ....1 tsp	Tomatoes .... 4 medium sized
Red chillies whole 12-15	Oil .... ½ cup
Cloves 10-12	Sugar .... 2 tbsps
Cinnamon .... 2 inch stick	Salt.. to taste

METHOD OF PREPARATION

1. De-vein prawns. Wash thoroughly under running water and remove excess water. Add salt and keep aside.

2. Peel and wash ginger and garlic.

3. Grind ginger, garlic, cumin seeds, whole red chillies, cloves, cinnamon and mustard seeds alongwith vinegar into a fine paste.

4. Peel, wash onions and chop finely. Wash and chop tomatoes.

5. Take oil and onions in a microwave bowl and cook, uncovered, on Microwave HIGH (100%) for four minutes. Add ground paste, tomatoes and cook, covered, on Microwave HIGH (100%) for four minutes.

6. Add prawns, salt and sugar and cook, covered, on Microwave HIGH (100%) for three minutes. Serve hot.

CHEF'S TIP

You need not use large sized prawns for this dish as Prawn Balchao tastes better with small sized prawns and it is economical too!

Prawns in Thai Red Curry Sauce

INGREDIENTS

Prawns .... 16 medium sized

Oil .... 2 tbsps

Lemon juice .... 1 tsp

Soy sauce .... 1 tsp

Coconut milk .... 1 cup

Fresh basil leaves 6-8

For red curry paste

Onion .... 1 medium sized

Garlic .... 4 cloves

Red chillies whole 8-10

Lemon grass stalk .... 4 inch piece

Coriander seeds .... 2 tsps

Cumin seeds .... 1 tsp

Peppercorns 6

Salt .... to taste

METHOD OF PREPARATION

1. Remove shells and de-vein prawns. Wash them thoroughly under running water. Drain and pat dry. Wash basil leaves.

2. For red curry paste, peel, wash and quarter onions. Peel garlic. Grind with the rest of the ingredients into a smooth paste using a little water.

3. In a deep microwave bowl, mix this paste with oil and three-fourth cup of water. Cook, uncovered, on Microwave HIGH (100%) for three minutes.

4. Stir in lemon juice, soy sauce and fresh basil leaves. Cook, uncovered, on Microwave HIGH (100%) for one minute.

5. Mix in prawns and coconut milk and cook, covered, on Microwave HIGH (100%) for three minutes. Adjust seasoning and serve hot.

Whole Wheat Vegetable Quiche

INGREDIENTS

For pastry

Whole wheat flour *(atta)* .... 1 cup
Salt .... a pinch
Butter .... ½ cup
Oil .... for greasing
Kidney beans *(rajmah)* .... ¼ cup

For filling

Carrot .... 1 medium sized
Zucchini .... ½ medium sized
Mushrooms 4-5

Capsicum .... 1 medium sized
Spring onion bulbs 2
Celery .... 2 stalks
Oil .... 1 tbsp
Milk .... 1 cup
Eggs 3
Processed cheese (grated) .... ½ cup
Salt... to taste
Pepper powder .... ¼ tsp

METHOD OF PREPARATION

1. Preheat Convection oven at 180° C. Grease a nine-inch pie dish with oil.

2. Sieve flour with salt and rub in chilled butter. Knead into a dough using three tablespoons of cold water. Do not knead too much or you will not get a proper texture in the finished product. Roll out on a floured surface to half a centimetre thickness and line the pie dish with it. Spread a grease proof paper (butter paper) on it and place some kidney beans (it prevents the sides from collapsing and the base from puffing up) on it and blind bake at 180° C in the preheated oven for fifteen minutes. Take out, remove kidney beans and paper.

3. Peel, wash and grate carrot. Wash zucchini and chop finely. Clean and wash mushrooms and slice. Wash, halve, de-seed capsicum and cut into half centimetre sized dices. Peel, wash spring onion and chop. Wash celery and cut into one centimetre sized pieces.

4. Place vegetables in a microwave casserole with oil. Cook, covered, on Microwave HIGH (100%) for three minutes.

5. Pour milk in another microwave bowl. Heat, covered, on Microwave HIGH (100%) for two minutes. Beat eggs and stir in milk, adding cheese and cooked vegetables. Add salt and pepper.

6. Pour this into the partly baked pastry and bake in the preheated oven at 180° C for twenty minutes. Cut into pieces and serve hot.

○ Convection and Microwave recipe

Speedy Egg Omelet

INGREDIENTS

Eggs	8	Milk	4 tbsps
Onions	2 medium sized	Salt	to taste
Green chillies	4-6	White pepper powder	¼ tsp
Fresh coriander leaves	a few sprigs	Butter	4 tbsps

METHOD OF PREPARATION

1. Peel, wash onions and chop finely. Remove stems, wash and finely chop green chillies.

2. Clean, wash and chop fresh coriander leaves.

3. Beat eggs and stir in onion, green chillies, coriander leaves, milk, salt and pepper. Divide the mixture into four equal portions.

4. Place one tablespoon of butter in a flat microwave dish and heat, uncovered, on Microwave HIGH (100%) for twenty seconds. Spread evenly and pour one portion of the egg mixture, ensuring that it spreads evenly too.

5. Cook, uncovered, on Microwave HIGH (100%) for three minutes. Allow standing time of one minute. Serve immediately. Repeat the process for the remaining omelets.

Tamarind Chutney

INGREDIENTS

Tamarind (seedless) .... 1 cup
Jaggery (grated) .... 1¼ cups
Cinnamon .... 1 inch stick
Black salt .... ½ tsp
Red chilli powder .... 1 tsp

Roasted cumin powder .... 1 tsp
Dry ginger powder .... 1½ tsps
Salt .... to taste
Raisins *(kishmish)* .... 2 tbsps

METHOD OF PREPARATION

1. Soak tamarind in two cups of water. Place in a microwave bowl and cook, uncovered, on Microwave HIGH (100%) for three minutes. Allow standing time of half an hour.

2. Extract pulp by straining through a sieve. Wash the raisins and pat them dry.

3. In a microwave bowl, mix jaggery, cinnamon and tamarind pulp. Cook, uncovered, on Microwave HIGH (100%) for twenty minutes.

4. Mix in black salt, red chilli powder, roasted cumin powder, dry ginger powder and salt to taste. Cook, uncovered, on Microwave HIGH (100%) for three minutes.

5. Add raisins and cook, uncovered, on Microwave HIGH (100%) for two minutes.

6. Let cool completely and store in an airtight container.

Sprouted Moong Kadhi

INGREDIENTS

Sprouted green gram (moong) .... ¾ cup	Red chillies whole 4
Ginger .... 1 inch piece	Peppercorns 6-8
Yogurt .... 1 cup	Oil .... 2 tbsps
Gram flour (besan) .... ¼ cup	Fenugreek seeds .... ½ tsp
Jaggery (grated) .... 1 tbsp	Cumin seeds .... ½ tsp
Salt .... to taste	Curry leaves 7-8
	Asafoetida .... ¼ tsp

METHOD OF PREPARATION

1. Place sprouted *moong* with two cups of water in a microwave bowl. Cover and cook on Microwave HIGH (100%) for five minutes. Drain any excess water. Keep aside.

2. Peel, wash and finely chop ginger.

3. Whisk together yogurt and gram flour thoroughly. Add two cups of water and mix well. Add jaggery and ginger.

4. Pour the above mixture into a deep microwave casserole and cook, covered, on Microwave HIGH (100%) for ten minutes, stirring once after five minutes. The mixture will turn to medium thick consistency. Remove and add salt to taste. Add cooked *moong* and cook further on Microwave HIGH (100%) for five minutes.

5. Break whole red chillies into two. Crush peppercorns coarsely.

6. Place oil in a microwave casserole. Add red chillies, peppercorns, fenugreek seeds, cumin seeds, curry leaves and asafoetida. Cook, uncovered, on Microwave HIGH (100%) for two minutes. Remove and add to the *kadhi*.

7. Serve hot with steamed rice.

Rajmah Masala

INGREDIENTS

Kidney beans (rajmah) .... 1 cup
Baking soda .... ¼ tsp
Onions .... 2 medium sized
Garlic .... 7 - 8 cloves
Ginger .... 1 inch piece
Tomatoes .... 4 medium sized
Green chillies 2-3

Fresh coriander leaves .... a few sprigs
Oil .... 4 tbsps
Red chilli powder .... 1 tsp
Coriander powder .... 2 tsps
Cumin powder............................ 1 tsp
Salt.. to taste
Garam masala powder .... 1½ tsps

METHOD OF PREPARATION

1. Soak the kidney beans overnight in four cups of water to which baking soda has been added. Drain, wash with fresh water and place in a deep microwave casserole with five cups of water and cook, covered, for nearly an hour on Microwave HIGH (100%). Stir every fifteen minutes. Press between your fingers to see if done.

2. Peel, wash and grind onions, garlic, ginger into a smooth paste. Wash tomatoes and make puree in a blender.

3. Wash, de-stem and finely chop green chillies. Clean, wash and chop coriander leaves.

4. Place oil with onion, garlic and ginger paste, green chillies in a microwave casserole and cook, uncovered, on Microwave HIGH (100%) for five minutes. Add red chilli powder, coriander powder, cumin powder and cook, uncovered, on Microwave HIGH (100%) for one minute.

5. Stir in the pureed tomato and cook, covered, on Microwave HIGH (100%) for eight minutes, stirring twice in between.

6. Stir in kidney beans with two cups of water and salt. Cook, covered, on Microwave HIGH (100%) for ten minutes. Remove and stir well.

7. Stir in garam masala powder. Finish with chopped coriander leaves. Serve hot with steamed rice.

Daily Dal

INGREDIENTS

Pigeon pea split *(toor/arhar dal)* .... ½ cup

Onions .... 2 medium sized

Tomatoes .... 3 medium sized

Garlic .... 2-4 cloves

Green chillies 2

Fresh coriander leaves .... a few sprigs

Red chillies whole 2-3

Salt .... to taste

Mustard seeds .... ½ tsp

Cumin seeds .... ½ tsp

Oil .... 2 tbsps

Asafoetida .... a pinch

METHOD OF PREPARATION

1. Soak *toor/arhar dal* for an hour. Drain.

2. Peel, wash and finely chop onions and keep aside. Wash and chop tomatoes. Peel and crush garlic. Remove stems, wash and slit green chillies. Clean, wash and finely chop coriander leaves. Break red chillies into two.

3. Cook the *dal* alongwith slit green chillies, onion, garlic, tomato, salt and four cups of water in a deep microwave bowl, covered, on Microwave HIGH (100%) for twenty-five minutes.

4. Stir the *dal* with a round spoon, mashing it slightly in the process.

5. In another microwave bowl take oil, mustard seeds, cumin seeds, whole red chillies and asafoetida. Cook, uncovered, on Microwave HIGH (100%) for three minutes.

6. Add the tempering to the cooked *dal*. Mix well. Serve hot sprinkled with chopped coriander leaves.

Mixed Fruit Chutney

INGREDIENTS

Almonds 15-16	Coriander seeds .... ½ tsp
Apple .... 1 large sized	Onion seeds *(kalonji)* .... ½ tsp
Plums 4	Aniseed .... ½ tsp
Mango 1	Cinnamon .... 1 inch stick
Dates .... 1 cup	Cider vinegar .... ¼ cup
Ginger .... 2 inch piece	Brown sugar or jaggery .... 1 cup
Pineapple .... 4 slices	Red chilli powder .... 1 tsp
Raisins *(kishmish)* .... ¼ cup	Salt .... to taste
Cumin seeds .... ½ tsp	

METHOD OF PREPARATION

1. Slice almonds. Wash, core and chop apple. Wash, stone and chop plums. Peel, wash and chop mango. Clean, stone and chop dates. Peel, wash and chop ginger. Cut pineapple slices into one centimetre sized cubes. Wash raisins and pat them dry.

2. Mix cumin seeds, coriander seeds, onion seeds, aniseed, cinnamon and almonds in a large, deep microwave bowl and cook, uncovered, on Microwave HIGH (100%) for five minutes to roast the spices and lightly brown the almonds.

3. Add the apple, plums, mango, dates, pineapple, raisins, ginger and vinegar. Cover and cook on Microwave HIGH (100%) for two minutes.

4. Add brown sugar or jaggery, red chilli powder and salt. Cook, covered, for a further twenty minutes on Microwave HIGH (100%), stirring occasionally.

> **NOTE**
>
> If the *chutney* becomes too thick during cooking, add the reserved pineapple juice. But if at the end of twenty minutes the *chutney* is not thick enough, uncover the bowl and continue to cook for another two to three minutes. Allow it to cool and pour into another container and refrigerate.

Pepper Chilli Sauce

INGREDIENTS

Green capsicums .... 3 medium sized
Tomatoes .... 6 medium sized
Onion .... 1 medium sized
Peppercorns 7-8
Cloves 4-5
Cinnamon .... 1 inch stick

Brown sugar .... ½ cup
Vinegar .... ¼ cup
Red chilli powder .... 1 tsp
Bay leaf 1
Salt .... to taste

METHOD OF PREPARATION

1. Wash, de-seed and cut capsicums into half centimetre sized cubes. Wash and chop tomatoes finely. Peel, wash and chop onion finely. Crush peppercorns.

2. Place cloves and cinnamon in a microwave plate and dry roast on Microwave HIGH (100%) for two minutes. Grind to a coarse powder.

3. Place tomatoes, onion, brown sugar, vinegar, clove-cinnamon powder, red chilli powder and bay leaf in a large microwave bowl. Cover and cook on Microwave HIGH (100%) for fifteen minutes.

4. Stir in capsicums, salt and add freshly crushed peppercorns. Cook, uncovered, on Microwave HIGH (100%) for fifteen minutes or until the mixture thickens.

5. Remove the bay leaf and pour sauce into hot, sterilized jars.

6. Seal and cover. Best stored in the refrigerator.

Sweet Chilli Sauce

INGREDIENTS

Kashmiri red chillies 18-20
Tomatoes .... 2 medium sized
Garlic .... 3-4 cloves
Sugar ....,,,,, 2 tbsps

Oil .... 1 tbsp
Soy sauce .... 1 tbsp
Salt .... to taste

METHOD OF PREPARATION

1. Remove stems and de-seed chillies. Wash and chop tomatoes. Peel and chop garlic. Grind all these together into a smooth paste.

2. Combine sugar and oil in a microwave casserole and cook, uncovered, on Microwave HIGH (100%) for two minutes.

3. Stir in paste, soy sauce, salt to taste and one cup of water. Mix well. Cook, uncovered, on Microwave HIGH (100%) for two minutes. Remove and stir once. Cook, uncovered, further for two minutes on Microwave HIGH (100%). Serve when cooled.

Quick Tomato Sauce

INGREDIENTS

Tomatoes .... 6 medium sized
Carrot .... 1 small sized
Onion .... 1 small sized
Garlic .... 6 - 8 cloves
Oil .... 2 tbsps

Basil leaves 10
Pepper powder .... 1 tsp
Salt .... to taste
Sugar .... ½ tsp

METHOD OF PREPARATION

1. Wash and cut tomatoes into quarters. Peel, wash and cut carrot into half centimetre sized cubes. Peel, wash and chop onion. Peel and crush garlic.

2. Heat oil in a microwave bowl, uncovered, for one minute on Microwave HIGH (100%). Remove, add carrot, garlic and onion. Cover and cook on Microwave HIGH (100%) for six minutes.

3. Add the tomatoes, basil, pepper powder, salt and sugar. Cover and cook on Microwave HIGH (100%) for six minutes, stirring halfway through the cooking time.

4. Remove and let it cool. Puree the mixture in a blender. Store in a glass bottle.

CHEF'S TIP
Use *tulsi* leaves to substitute basil leaves in the above recipe.

Wholemeal Bread

INGREDIENTS

Whole wheat flour (*atta*) .... 3 cups (350 gms)
Refined flour (*maida*) .... 1 cup (120 gms)
Milk .... 1¼ cups
Fresh yeast .... 1½ tbsps
Vegetable *ghee* .... 2 tbsps
Brown sugar .... 1 tbsp
Salt........................... .... 2 tsps
Oil .... for greasing

METHOD OF PREPARATION

1. Prepare a loaf tin by greasing it with oil and dusting it with a little flour.

2. Place fresh yeast in a small bowl with sugar and a quarter cup of water.

3. Sift *maida*, *atta* and salt together. Make a well in the centre, pour the yeast mixture into it. Bring in some of the flour from the sides into the centre and swiftly make a paste. Cover with the remaining flour and keep as it is, covered, for fifteen minutes to ferment.

4. Add milk and knead into a soft dough. Add *ghee* and work it into the dough.

5. Dust a fresh bowl with some flour and keep the dough in it, covered with a damp muslin cloth, to ferment for an hour and a half. Knead back and rest for further ten minutes.

6. Shape the dough like a pillow and place it in the prepared loaf tin, covering it again with a damp muslin cloth. Allow it to rise for thirty minutes or till it is double in size.

7. Preheat Convection oven at 230°C.

8. Bake in the preheated oven at 230°C for an hour. To check if it is done, knock at the bottom with a spoon. If it sounds hollow, that means the bread is done. Remove the tin from the oven and allow it to cool on a wire rack.

NOTE

Good kneading is very essential because it blends the ingredients and stretches the gluten in the flour thus enabling the dough to rise well and make the bread soft.

CHEF'S TIP

Bran can also be added to the wholemeal flour while making brown bread. It will make it more nutritious.

○ Convection recipe

Basic Pizza Bread

INGREDIENTS

Refined flour *(maida)* .... 1½ cups

Dried yeast .... 1½ tsps

Sugar .... 1 tsp

Salt .... 1 tsp

Oil .... 1½ tbsps

METHOD OF PREPARATION

1. Take one-fourth cup of water and heat on Microwave HIGH (100%) for half a minute.

2. Mix yeast with warm water and sugar and leave aside until frothy.

3. Add frothy yeast to refined flour. Add salt and one tablespoon of oil and mix. Add approximately half a cup of water more and knead into a soft dough.

4. Leave the dough covered with a damp cloth in a warm place for about forty-five minutes or until the dough is about double in volume.

5. Knead the dough again and keep for ten to fifteen minutes covered with a moist muslin cloth.

6. Preheat the Convection oven to 200°C.

7. Divide the pizza dough into four, roll out each portion into medium thick, eight inch diameter discs. Prick them with a fork all over. Grease a baking tray with a little oil and place the pizza bases over it.

8. Bake them in the preheated oven for eight minutes.

○ Convection recipe

Bread Sticks

INGREDIENTS

Refined flour (*maida*) .... 1 cup
Salt .... ½ tsp
Dry yeast .... 1½ tsps
Sugar .... ½ tsp
Vegetable *ghee* .... 1¼ tsps

Egg .... 1 (optional)
Sesame seeds/onion seeds/poppy
seeds .... as required
Oil .... for greasing

METHOD OF PREPARATION

1. Pour three-fourth cup of water in a microwave bowl and heat on Microwave LOW (40%) for two minutes.

2. Place yeast and sugar in a cup. Pour lukewarm water over this.

3. Sift refined flour and salt together. Place in a large mixing bowl. Make a well in the center of the flour.

4. Pour the yeast liquid into the well in the flour and mix. Rub in the softened fat (*ghee*) to form a smooth but a fairly firm dough, using extra water if needed, kneading lightly for ten minutes. Cover with a moist cloth and rest until double in size. Knead back the dough, allow it to rest for further ten minutes and then roll it into a rectangle about one-fourth inch thick on a lightly floured work surface.

5. Preheat the Convection oven to 230°C.

6. Cut the rolled dough into one centimetre by eight centimetre strips. Take individual strips and roll into ten to twelve centimetre long sticks.

7. Place them on a greased baking tray. Beat egg with fork lightly. Brush the bread sticks with egg and sprinkle them with sesame seeds/onion seeds/poppy seeds.

8. Bake in the preheated oven at 230°C for fifteen minutes and then reduce the temperature to 190°C and bake for another ten minutes.

9. Remove, cool and store in an air-tight container.

CHEF'S TIP

Sea salt, dried herbs or carom seeds can be sprinkled on top of Grissini (bread stick) to give it that extra zing.

○ Convection recipe

Spinach & Mushroom Risotto

INGREDIENTS

Parboiled rice .... 1½ cups	White wine .... 1 cup
Onion .... 1 medium sized	Vegetable stock* or water .... 3½ cups
Garlic .... 4-5 cloves	Salt .... to taste
Fresh mushrooms 4-5	Parmesan cheese (grated) .... ¾ cup
Spinach .... ½ bunch	Pepper powder .... ½ tsp
Butter .... 5 tbsps	Fresh cream .... ½ cup

METHOD OF PREPARATION

1. Wash and soak rice in just enough water to cover it for two hours. Drain water and keep aside. Peel, wash and chop onion. Peel and finely chop garlic. Clean, wash and slice mushrooms.

2. Clean, wash spinach thoroughly under running water and roughly chop.

3. Mix three tablespoons of butter, onion, garlic and mushrooms in a deep microwave casserole. Cook, uncovered, on Microwave HIGH (100%) for three minutes.

4. Add rice, wine, half of the stock and salt and cook on Microwave HIGH (100%) for ten minutes.

5. Stir in the remaining stock and cook for another ten minutes on Microwave HIGH (100%).

6. Stir in the cheese, pepper powder, spinach, cream and mix well. Cook, uncovered, on Microwave HIGH (100%) for two minutes. Mix in the remaining two tablespoons of butter and finish. Serve hot.

NOTE
*Refer page no. 124 for the recipe of Vegetable Stock.

Chilli Paneer Stuffed Croissants

INGREDIENTS

For croissant

Refined flour (maida)	4 cups+for dusting
Milk powder	2½ tbsps
Salt	2 tsps
Fresh yeast	1 tbsp
Sugar	3 tbsps
Butter	1¼ cups
Egg	1

For stuffing

Cottage cheese (paneer)	100 gms
Cornstarch	¾ tbsp
Salt	to taste
Soy sauce	½ tbsp
Chilli sauce	½ tbsp
Onion	1 small sized
Garlic	2-3 cloves
Green chillies	2-3
Capsicum	½ medium sized
Peppercorns	3-4
Oil	1 tsp
Ajinomoto	a pinch
Vinegar	½ tbsp

METHOD OF PREPARATION

For the dough

1. In a bowl mix together flour, milk powder and salt. Dissolve yeast and sugar in half a cup of water and allow it to stand for fifteen minutes. Keep butter in the deep freezer for chilling.

2. Add the yeast mixture to the flour. Add three-fourth cup of chilled water and knead into a smooth dough. Keep the dough, covered with a damp muslin cloth, in a warm place to rise for thirty to forty minutes.

3. Slice the chilled butter into thin slices.

4. Knead back the dough and roll it into a forty centimetre by seventy centimetre rectangle using a little flour for dusting. Brush off the excess flour.

5. Arrange the chilled butter slices on two-third portion of the rectangle. Fold the uncovered one-third part over to the centre and bring over the remaining one-third part to make a book fold. Seal the sides well so that the butter does not come out.

6. Roll the pastry again to the same size and make a book fold. Keep it in the refrigerator for half an hour covered in a cling film so that no moisture gets in.

7. Repeat the process twice without the butter. Again roll the dough into a rectangle of the same size and trim the sides.

8. Cut it into two strips, lengthwise, with a sharp knife and then cut into big triangles with each side measuring approximately fifteen centimetres.

For the stuffing

9. Cut the *paneer* into one centimetre sized cubes. Mix half of the cornstarch, salt, half of the soy sauce and half of the chilli sauce and leave the *paneer* pieces to marinate in it for half an hour.

10. Peel, wash and chop onion finely. Peel and finely chop garlic. Remove stems, wash and chop green chillies finely. Wash, halve, deseed and cut capsicum into one centimetre sized cubes. Blend the remaining cornstarch in two tablespoons of water. Crush peppercorns.

11. Take one teaspoon of oil in a microwave bowl, add garlic, onion and green chillies. Cook, uncovered, on Microwave HIGH (100%) for two minutes.

12. Add the capsicum and cook, uncovered, on Microwave HIGH (100%) for two minutes. Add the remaining soy sauce and chilli sauce, ajinomoto, salt, crushed peppercorns and blended cornstarch. Cover and cook on Microwave HIGH (100%) for two minutes.

13. Add the marinated *paneer* pieces and cook, uncovered, on Microwave MEDIUM (70%) for two minutes. Add vinegar and keep aside to cool.

To make the croissants

14. Preheat the oven to Convection 210°C.

15. Place the dough triangles on a lightly floured surface. Place one tablespoon of *paneer* mixture on the base of the triangle. Roll it in the shape of a crescent.

16. Place them on a baking tray, lightly brush them with an egg glaze and leave to rise in a warm, humid place for thirty minutes till doubled in size.

17. Bake the croissants in the preheated oven for fifteen minutes. Reduce the temperature to 190°C and further bake for ten minutes. Serve hot immediately.

Steamed Rice

INGREDIENTS

Basmati Rice .... 1½ cups   Salt .... to taste

METHOD OF PREPARATION

1. Wash and soak rice in sufficient water for one hour.

2. Drain and transfer to a large microwave bowl. Add three cups of water, salt and stir well. Cover and cook for thirteen minutes on Microwave HIGH (100%).

3. Allow standing time in the microwave itself for five minutes before serving.

Sabz Biryani

INGREDIENTS

Basmati rice .... 1½ cups	Cloves 4-5
Green peas (shelled) .... ½ cup	Cinnamon .... 1 inch stick
Carrot .... 1 medium sized	Bayleaf 1
Cauliflower .... ¼ small sized	Yogurt .... ½ cup
French beans 4-5	Red chilli powder .... 1 tsp
Onions .... 3 medium sized	Coriander powder .... 1 tbsp
Tomatoes .... 2 medium sized	Turmeric powder .... ½ tsp
Green chillies 2	Salt .... to taste
Ginger .... 1 inch piece	**For garnish**
Fresh coriander leaves .... a few sprigs	Fresh mint leaves .... a few sprigs
Ghee .... 3 tbsps	Saffron .... 4-5 strands
Cumin seeds .... 1 tsp	Milk .... ¼ cup
Black cardamoms 2	Oil .... 2 tbsps
Green cardamoms 4	*Kewra* water .... a few drops

METHOD OF PREPARATION

1. Wash rice twice and soak in just enough water to cover it for half an hour. Drain off excess water.

2. Wash green peas. Peel, wash and chop carrot. Wash and separate cauliflower into small florets. String, wash and chop French beans. Peel, wash and chop one onion and slice the other two. Wash and chop tomatoes. Remove stems, wash and chop green chillies. Peel, wash and chop ginger. Clean, wash and chop coriander leaves finely.

3. Place rice in a microwave casserole with five cups of water and salt to taste. Cook, covered, on Microwave HIGH (100%) for ten minutes. Remove, drain and keep aside.

4. In a separate microwave bowl place sliced onions with two tablespoons of oil. Cook, uncovered, on Microwave HIGH (100%) for four minutes. Remove and drain the onion onto an absorbent paper.

5. Soak saffron in milk. Clean, wash and roughly chop the mint leaves.

6. Take a large microwave casserole. Place three tablespoons of *ghee* with chopped onion, ginger, cumin seeds, green chillies, black cardamoms, green cardamoms, cloves, cinnamon and bay leaf. Cook, uncovered, on Microwave HIGH (100%) for three minutes.

7. Mix in peas, carrot, cauliflower, French beans, tomatoes, coriander leaves, yogurt, red chilli powder, coriander powder, turmeric powder, salt to taste with one and a half cups of water. Cook, covered, on Microwave HIGH (100%) for twelve minutes.

8. In another large microwave casserole, place half of the vegetables and cover them with half of the rice. Repeat the layers. Cook, covered, on Microwave HIGH (100%) for twenty minutes.

9. Sprinkle saffron, cooked sliced onions, mint leaves and *kewra* water on rice and cook, covered, on Microwave HIGH (100%) for ten minutes. Serve hot.

Chicken Pulao

INGREDIENTS

Basmati rice	1¼ cups	Green cardamoms	3
Chicken (boneless)	250 gms	Cinnamon	1 inch stick
Onion	1 medium sized	Cumin seeds	½ tsp
Tomatoes	2 medium sized	Bay leaf	1
Yogurt	¼ cup	Cloves	3
Ginger paste	2 tbsps	Red chilli powder	1 tsp
Garlic paste	2 tbsps	Chicken stock* or water	2 cups
Salt	to taste	*Kewra* water	1 tsp
Ghee	2 tbsps		

METHOD OF PREPARATION

1. Wash rice twice and soak in just enough water to cover it for an hour. Drain off water and keep aside.

2. Wash chicken well and drain. Cut into one and a half inch sized cubes.

3. Peel, wash and slice the onion. Wash and chop tomatoes.

4. Beat together yogurt, ginger paste and garlic paste. Add chicken and salt to taste. Keep to marinate for one hour.

5. Mix *ghee*, green cardamoms, cinnamon, cumin seeds, bay leaf, cloves and onion in a microwave casserole. Cook, uncovered, on Microwave HIGH (100%) for two minutes.

6. Add tomatoes and red chilli powder. Cook, uncovered, on Microwave HIGH (100%) for five minutes.

7. Add chicken with marinade. Cover and cook on Microwave HIGH (100%) for three minutes.

8. Add rice and chicken stock and cover again. Cook on Microwave HIGH (100%) for fifteen minutes. Allow standing time of five minutes.

9. Just before serving sprinkle with *kewra* water.

NOTE

*Refer page no. 125 for the recipe of Chicken Stock.

CHEF'S TIP

You can also use chicken with bones to make this *pulao*.

Acharya Khichdi

INGREDIENTS

Rice	1 cup	Ghee	2 tbsps
Green gram split (moong dal)	¾ cup	Cloves	4
Carrot	½ medium sized	Cinnamon	1 inch stick
Potato	1 medium sized	Turmeric powder	⅛ tsp
Tomatoes	2 medium sized	Red chilli powder	1 tsp
French beans	4-5	Cumin seeds	1 tsp
		Salt	to taste

METHOD OF PREPARATION

1. Wash rice and *moong dal* together. Soak in just enough water to cover for an hour. Drain off water and keep aside.

2. Peel and wash carrot and potato and cut into half inch sized cubes. Wash tomatoes and cut into half inch sized dices. String, wash and cut French beans into half inch sized pieces.

3. In a large microwave casserole, place rice, *moong dal*, carrot, potato, French beans, tomatoes, *ghee*, cloves, cinnamon, turmeric powder, red chilli powder, cumin seeds, salt and pour four cups of water. Stir once, cover and cook on Microwave HIGH (100%) for twenty minutes. Serve hot.

CHEF'S TIP

This dish is named thus because it is served as a one dish meal in *gurukuls* or temples. The teacher in *gurukuls* is referred to as Acharya.

Farm House Fruit Cake

INGREDIENTS

Refined flour *(maida)* .... 2¼ cups

Mixed dry fruits (cashewnuts, raisins) ....

.... ½ cup

Eggs 3

Baking powder .... ½ tsp

Cinnamon powder .... ½ tsp

Oil .... ½ cup

Brown sugar .... ¾ cup

Milk .... ¾ cup

Honey .... 1 tbsp

METHOD OF PREPARATION

1. Roughly chop cashewnuts. Wash and dry raisins. Beat eggs. Grease an eight inch by three inch rectangular cake tin and lightly dust it with flour. Preheat a Convection oven to 180°C.

2. Mix flour with baking powder and cinnamon powder and sift into a mixing bowl. Rub in oil, until the mixture resembles fine breadcrumbs.

3. Add sugar and mixed dry fruits into the flour mixture.

4. In a jug, mix together the milk, eggs and honey. Add to the flour mixture. Mix well.

5. Pour into the prepared cake tin and bake in the preheated oven at 180°C for forty-five minutes. Test by inserting a skewer or knife, it should come out clean.

6. Remove from oven and let cool in the tin for five minutes before turning out. Cut into slices and serve.

O Convection recipe

Kalakand

INGREDIENTS

Milk .... 5 cups
Tartaric powder .... ¼ tsp
Sugar .... ¾ cup
Cornstarch .... 1 tsp

For garnish

Green cardamom powder .... 1 tsp
Pistachios 5-6

METHOD OF PREPARATION

1. Place pistachios in a small glass bowl with half a cup of water. Cook, uncovered, on Microwave HIGH (100%) for five minutes. Drain, peel and slice pistachios.

2. Place milk in a deep microwave casserole and cook, uncovered, on Microwave HIGH (100%) for ten minutes. Cool for five minutes, add tartaric powder and stir in sugar. Cook, uncovered, on Microwave HIGH (100%) for ten minutes. The milk will curdle slowly. Tiny granules will stick to the back of the spoon on stirring.

3. Pass the curdled milk through a moist muslin cloth and collect the solids. Pass the milk solids through a sieve and sprinkle cornstarch.

4. Spread mixture on a microwave plate giving half centimetre height and cook, uncovered, on Microwave HIGH (100%) for four minutes.

5. Sprinkle with cardamom powder and pistachios. Allow to cool. Once set, cut into pieces and serve.

Gajar Halwa

INGREDIENTS

Carrots	8-10 medium sized	Green cardamom powder	¼ tsp
Milk	2 cups	Cashewnuts	8-10
Khoya (grated)	1 cup	Raisins *(kishmish)*	10-15
Sugar	¾ cup	Almonds	4-5
Pure *ghee*	3 tbsps	Silver *varq*	1 sheet

METHOD OF PREPARATION

1. Wash, peel and grate carrots. To steam them in their own moisture cover and cook in a deep casserole on Microwave HIGH (100%) for ten minutes.

2. Wash raisins and pat them dry. Place almonds in a small glass bowl with one fourth cup of water. Cook, uncovered, on Microwave High (100%) for two minutes. Drain, peel and slice almonds.

3. Add milk to the cooked carrots, cover and cook on Microwave HIGH (100%) for eight minutes. Allow standing time of five minutes.

4. Stir well, add *khoya* and sugar and stir again. Cover and cook on Microwave HIGH (100%) for eight more minutes. Allow standing time of three minutes.

5. Add *ghee* and green cardamom powder. Mix well, cover and cook further on Microwave HIGH (100%) for ten minutes.

6. Garnish with chopped cashewnuts, sliced almonds and raisins. Cover and cook on Microwave HIGH (100%) for five minutes.

7. Decorate with silver *varq* and serve hot or cold.

NOTE
To serve hot, reheat on Microwave HIGH (100%) for one minute before serving. Sweetened condensed milk can be used in place of milk and sugar to reduce cooking time.

CHEF'S TIP
Use Dilli Gajar (they are more red and sweet) when in season for they give the best results.

Chocolate Brownies

INGREDIENTS

Dark cooking chocolate .... 100 gms
Refined flour *(maida)* .... 1 cup
Baking powder .... 1 tsp
Walnuts (shelled) .... ½ cup
Butter .... 90 gms

Castor sugar .... 1 cup
Eggs 2
Vanilla essence .... 1 tsp
Oil .... for greasing

METHOD OF PREPARAION

1. Sift the flour and baking powder and keep aside. Chop the walnuts. Grease a round microwave dish and line it with butter paper.

2. Combine chocolate and butter in a large microwave bowl and soften, uncovered, on Microwave HIGH (100%) for one minute.

3. Beat in sugar, eggs and vanilla essence and blend well. Add the sifted flour and nuts and mix well.

4. Pour the entire mixture into the greased and lined dish. Place the dish on an upturned saucer and cook, uncovered, on Microwave HIGH (100%) for seven minutes. Allow standing time of five minutes.

5. Insert a skewer, if it comes out clean then the brownies are done. If not, cook uncovered, on Microwave MEDIUM (60%) for two more minutes.

6. Place on a wire rack to cool. Cut into squares and serve with tea or coffee.

> **CHEF'S TIP**
> The baking dish is kept over an inverted saucer in order to allow the air to circulate underneath. This allows the base to cook more evenly.

Choconut Fudge

INGREDIENTS

Dark chocolate .... 100 gms
Mixed nuts (cashewnuts, almonds, ...
pistachios) .... ½ cup
Butter (unsalted) .... 4 tbsps

Milk .... 2 tbsps
Vanilla essence .... ½ tsp
Icing sugar .... 1 cup

METHOD OF PREPARATION

1. Chop the cashewnuts, almonds and pistachios fine.

2. Break the chocolate into small pieces. Cut the butter into small pieces and place both in a deep microwave dish.

3. Cook, uncovered, on Microwave HIGH (100%) for one minute. Remove and stir. Cook, uncovered, for another two minutes or till the chocolate melts completely and bubbles.

4. Stir in milk and vanilla essence into the chocolate mixture. Mix in the icing sugar gradually, stirring continuously. Add nuts and mix well.

5. Pour into a shallow serving dish and cool in the refrigerator for fifteen to twenty minutes or till it sets. Remove and cut into cubes.

Rice Kheer

INGREDIENTS

Rice	¼ cup	Saffron	a pinch
Cashewnuts	10-12	Milk	5 cups
Raisins *(kishmish)*	12-14	Sugar	5 tbsps
Green cardamom powder	½ tsp		

METHOD OF PREPARATION

1. Pick, wash and soak rice for two hours in one cup of water. Drain and keep aside. Split cashewnuts into two. Wash and dry raisins. Soak saffron strands in one tablespoon of warm milk.

2. Pour milk in a deep microwave casserole, cover and bring to boil on Microwave HIGH (100%) for twenty-five minutes.

3. Add the rice and stir. Cover and cook for ten minutes on Microwave MEDIUM (70%), check whether the rice is cooked.

4. Add sugar and mix well. Cover and cook on Microwave MEDIUM (70%) for five minutes.

5. Add green cardamom powder, saffron, cashewnuts and raisins. Cover and cook again for five minutes on Microwave MEDIUM (70%).

6. Serve hot or chilled.

CHEF'S TIP

In order to ensure that rice gets cooked completely, sugar should be added after it is cooked.

Créme Caramel

INGREDIENTS

Caramel

Sugar .... ¼ cup

Custard

Eggs 4-5

Milk .... 2 ½ cups

Sugar .... ½ cup

Vanilla essence .... few drops

Nutmeg powder .... ¼ tsp

METHOD OF PREPARATION

1. To make caramel, take sugar and one tablespoon of water in a microwave bowl and cook, uncovered, on Microwave HIGH (100%) for one and a half to two minutes or till it caramalises. Pour into a mould. Allow to cool and set.

2. Put milk in a bowl and heat on Microwave HIGH (100%) for five minutes. Allow it to cool slightly.

3. Preheat the Convection oven to 200°C.

4. In a bowl break eggs, add sugar and whisk gently to blend well.

5. Add warm milk and vanilla essence and mix again stirring gently.

6. Strain this mixture and pour into the mould with the caramel. Sprinkle nutmeg powder. Cover the mould with a foil.

7. Cook in the preheated oven for forty five minutes. To check if it is done, test by inserting a skewer or knife. It should come out clean. Allow standing time of ten to fifteen minutes. Unmould on a serving plate. Can be served hot or cold.

O Convection recipe

Sooji aur Badam Halwa

INGREDIENTS

Semolina (*rava, suji*) .... 1 cup	Milk .... 6 cups
Almonds .... 1 cup	Saffron .... few strands
Ghee .... ½ cup	Green cardamom powder .... 1½ tsps
Sugar .... 2 cups	

METHOD OF PREPARATION

1. Place the semolina in a microwave dish and roast, uncovered, on Microwave HIGH (100%) for three minutes.

2. Place almonds in a glass bowl in one and a half cups of water. Cook, uncovered, on Microwave HIGH (100%) for three minutes. Drain, refresh in cold water and peel. Place in a microwave dish and cook, uncovered, on Microwave HIGH (100%) for three minutes, they should be crisp. Remove, let cool and chop. Reserve some for garnishing.

3. Mix *ghee* and roasted semolina in a deep microwave casserole. Cover and cook on Microwave HIGH (100%) for three minutes.

4. Stir well and add sugar, milk, saffron and green cardamom powder. Cover and cook on Microwave HIGH (100%) for five minutes.

5. Add chopped almonds, reduce the power to Microwave LOW (40%) and cook, uncovered, for twelve minutes or until thickened.

6. Stir well. Sprinkle the reserved almonds on top and serve hot.

Cabinet Pudding
with
Easy Strawberry Sauce

INGREDIENTS

Eggs 5

Sugar .... ¾ cup

Vanilla essence .... 2-3 drops

Milk .... 2½ cups

Raisins *(kishmish)* .... ½ cup

Candied orange peel .... 1 small segment

Walnut kernels .... ¼ cup

Sponge cake .... 4 slices

Butter .... 1 tsp

For strawberry sauce

Strawberry jam .... ¾ cup

Cherries 16-18

METHOD OF PREPARATION

1. Break eggs in a bowl and combine gently with sugar and vanilla essence.

2. Take milk in a microwave bowl and heat on Microwave HIGH (100%) for a minute. Mix milk and egg mixture using a wire whisk. Strain and keep aside.

3. Wash and pat dry raisins. Chop candied orange peel and walnut kernels. Cut cake into one inch sized pieces. Preheat Convection oven to 200°C.

4. Butter four ovenproof dessert bowls and sprinkle with chopped nuts and cake.

5. Gently pour the egg-milk mixture. Cover with foil.

6. Pour hot water in a large baking dish. Place dessert bowls in this. Bake in the preheated oven for forty five to fifty minutes. Check if done by inserting a skewer or knife, it should come out clean. Remove and let cool completely. Serve individual moulds topped with strawberry sauce.

7. For strawberry sauce mix strawberry jam with one cup of water in a microwave bowl. Cook, covered, on Microwave HIGH (100%) for six minutes, stirring once after three minutes. Add cherries and cook, covered, on Microwave HIGH (100%) for two minutes.

Zafrani Pulao

INGREDIENTS

Long grain rice	2 cups	Nutmeg powder	¼ tsp
Almonds	20	Green cardamom powder	½ tsp
Cashewnuts	12	Sugar	½ cup
Ghee	4 tbsp	Milk	¼ cup
Saffron	a pinch	Raisins (kishmish)	25-30

METHOD OF PREPARATION

1. Wash rice twice and soak in just enough water to cover it for half an hour. Drain excess water.

2. Place cashewnuts in a flat microwave dish and cook, uncovered, on Microwave MEDIUM (70%) for five minutes. Place almonds in a small glass bowl with half a cup of water. Cook, uncovered, on Microwave High (100%) for three minutes. Drain, peel and slice almonds. Halve the cashewnuts.

3. In a deep casserole, mix ghee and rice and cook, uncovered, on Microwave HIGH (100%) for two minutes. Stir. Cook, uncovered, on Microwave HIGH (100%) for two minutes more.

4. Mix nutmeg powder, green cardamom powder, saffron, raisins and sugar into the rice.

5. Add three and a half cups of water and milk and stir once.

6. Cover and cook on Microwave HIGH (100%) for fifteen minutes. Allow standing time of five minutes.

7. Garnish with almonds and cashewnuts. Serve hot.

Chocolate Turtle Cheese Cake

INGREDIENTS

Milk chocolate	200 gms	Sugar	½ cup
Butter	4 tbsps	Vanilla essence	1 tsp
Biscuit crumbs	1¼ cups	Eggs	2
Milk powder	½ cup	Milk	2 tbsps
Almonds	¾ cup	**For caramel**	
Cream cheese	450 gms	Sugar	½ cup

METHOD OF PREPARATION

1. Put butter in a nine inch round microwave glass cake pan. Heat on Microwave HIGH (100%) for forty seconds, until melted. Stir in biscuit crumbs and pat onto the bottom of the pan.

2. Put sugar and four tablespoons of water together in a glass bowl and cook, uncovered, on Microwave HIGH (100%) for three minutes to make caramel. Add milk powder to the caramel. Mix and pour over the crumbs.

3. Roast almonds in a microwave dish on Microwave HIGH (100%) for two minutes turning once. Allow them to cool. Keep aside ten to twelve pieces and crush the rest lightly with a rolling pin.

4. Sprinkle the crushed almonds on the caramel and press lightly. Refrigerate. Grate chocolate.

5. Put cream cheese in a large microwave glass mixing bowl with half of the grated chocolate. Cook, uncovered, on Microwave MEDIUM (50%) for three minutes, until the cheese is softened and chocolate has melted. Add sugar and vanilla essence, blend with an electric beater. Add eggs and blend. Pour on top of the caramel layer in the cake pan.

6. Cook, covered, on Microwave MEDIUM (70%) for ten minutes rotating twice while it is being cooked. The centre should jiggle slightly. Cool and refrigerate.

7. Combine the remaining chocolate and milk in a microwave bowl. Cook, covered, on Microwave HIGH (100%) for two minutes, until chocolate has melted. Stir until smooth and spread on top of cheesecake. Top with the remaining roasted almonds.

NOTE

Assembled cheesecake can be baked in a pre-heated Convection oven at 180°C for forty minutes.

Irish Coffee

INGREDIENTS

Irish whisky (or Irish mist liqueur) .... ½ cup

Instant coffee powder .... 3 tsps

Sugar .... 4 tsps

Heavy cream (chilled) .... ¼ cup

METHOD OF PREPARATION

1. Add two teaspoons of sugar to the chilled cream and whip till it forms peaks. Keep aside.

2. Pour three cups of water in a deep microwave bowl, cover. Place on Microwave HIGH (100%) for five minutes or until steaming. Remove, add coffee powder and the remaining two teaspoons of sugar. Stir to dissolve it. Pour in whisky/liqueur gently.

3. Pour coffee into four stemmed glasses and top it with whipped cream.

Vegetable Stock

INGREDIENTS

Onion	1 medium sized	Bayleaf	1
Carrot	½ medium sized	Peppercorns	5-6
Celery	2-3 inch stalk	Cloves	2-3
Garlic	2 cloves		

METHOD OF PREPARATION

1. Peel, wash and slice onion and carrot. Wash and cut celery into small pieces. Peel and crush garlic.

2. Take all the above ingredients in a deep microwave pan along with bayleaf, peppercorns and cloves. Add five cups of water and cook on Microwave HIGH (100%) for eight minutes.

3. Strain and use.

Chicken Stock

INGREDIENTS

Chicken bones	200 gms.	Peppercorns	6-7
Onion	1 medium sized	Cloves	5-6
Carrot	1 medium sized	Bayleaf	1

METHOD OF PREPARATION

1. Wash and clean bones in hot water, remove any excess fat.

2. Peel, wash and cut onion into quarters. Wash and cut carrot into two-three large pieces.

3. Put chicken bones, onion, carrot, peppercorns, cloves and bayleaf in a large microwave casserole with ten cups of water and cook, uncovered, on Microwave HIGH (100%) for twenty five minutes or till the quantity is reduced to half. Strain and use.

White Sauce

INGREDIENTS

Refined flour *(maida)* .... 1½ tbsps
Butter .... 2 tbsps
Onion........................... 1 medium sized
Bayleaf 1
Cloves 2

Milk .... 1 ½ cups
Nutmeg powder .... a small pinch
Salt.................................. to taste
White pepper powder .... ¼ tsp

METHOD OF PREPARATION

1. Peel and wash onion. Wrap a bayleaf around it studding it with cloves at two ends. Place milk in a deep bowl, place the onion in that and boil on Microwave HIGH (100%) for two minutes. Remove onion and keep aside.

2. Take butter and refined flour in a casserole and cook on Microwave HIGH (100%) for two minutes stirring once in between. Add milk, mix and cook further on Microwave MEDIUM (70%) for five minutes stirring once in between. Add nutmeg powder, salt and white pepper powder and stir.

Sichuan Sauce

INGREDIENTS

Red chillies whole 20
Green chillies 2
Spring onions 3
Ginger .... 1½ inch piece
Garlic .... 14 cloves
Celery .... 2-3 inches stalk
Oil .... ¼ cup

Vegetable stock* or water .... ¼ cup
Tomato ketchup .... 5 tbsps
Salt .... to taste
Sugar .... 1 tsp
Ajinomoto .... 1 tsp
Vinegar .... 3 tsps

METHOD OF PREPARATION

1. Remove stems of red chillies. Remove stems, wash and finely chop green chillies. Peel, wash and finely chop spring onions. Wash and finely chop some of the spring onion greens. Peel, wash and grate ginger. Peel and wash garlic. Finely chop two cloves of garlic. Wash and finely chop celery stalk.

2. Take one cup of water and red chillies in a Microwave bowl, cover and cook on Microwave HIGH (100%) for four to five minutes.

3. Grind the red chillies and the remaining cloves of garlic to a fine paste.

4. Heat oil in a microwave bowl, uncovered, for two minutes on Microwave HIGH (100%). Add chopped garlic, green chillies, spring onion and grated ginger. Cover and cook on Microwave HIGH (100%) for two to three minutes.

5. Add the red chillies and garlic paste, vegetable stock or water, celery, tomato ketchup, salt, sugar, ajinomoto and stir to blend well. Cover and cook on Microwave HIGH (100%) for two to three minutes.

6. Add vinegar and chopped spring onion greens. Cover and cook on Microwave Medium (70%) for one minute.

7. Cool and store.

NOTE
*Refer page no.124 for the recipe of Vegetable Stock

Fish Stock

INGREDIENTS

Fish bones, head, skin .... 200 gms
Onion .... 1 medium sized
Celery .... 2-3 inch stalk
Mushroom .... 1 large
Bay leaf 1
Peppercorns 4-6

METHOD OF PREPARATION

1. Wash fish bones, head and skin. Peel, wash and slice onion, wash and cut celery into one centimeter pieces, wash and slice mushroom.

2. Take five cups of water in a Microwave bowl and add fish bones, head, skin (any unutilised portion of fish), onion slices, mushroom slices, celery pieces, bay leaf and peppercorns and cook covered on Microwave HIGH (100%) for five minutes.

3. Strain and use the liquid as stock.

CHEF'S TIP

Fish stock should not be stored in the refrigerator as it smells and affects other food.

Subscribe to the most acclaimed food site
www.sanjeevkapoor.com and avail of unbelievable offers!!!

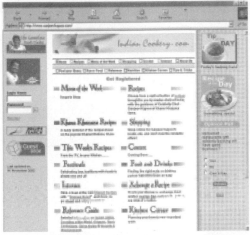

Pay Rs.600* only for one year subscription instead of normal subscription charges of Rs. 1000/- and get Sanjeev Kapoor Books worth Rs. 750/- FREE
(only upto 31st December, 2003).
You will also have access to more than 1000 recipes other than those published in his books besides many other sections, which will be a rare culinary treat to any food lover. In addition to online contests, etc. you will also have opportunities to win fabulous prizes.

Sanjeev Kapoor also invites all food lovers to participate in the Khana Khazana Quiz and win BIG prizes every week. Watch *Khana Khazana* on Zee IV, answer one simple question based on that day's episode correctly, combine it with a favourite recipe of yours and you can be the lucky winner going places.

*Add Service tax Rs. 48.00

Normal Subscription	You Pay	Plus You Get	You Save
Rs 1,000.	Rs 600 (add service tax Rs. 48/-)	Sanjeev Kapoor's books worth Rs 750 free.	Rs 1,150.

*Offer open only up to December 31st, 2003

**Delivery address for free books must be in India.

The three books free with each subscription are

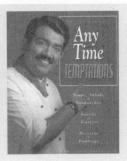

☐ Yes, I would like to subscribe to <u>www.sanjeevkapoor.com</u> for one year.

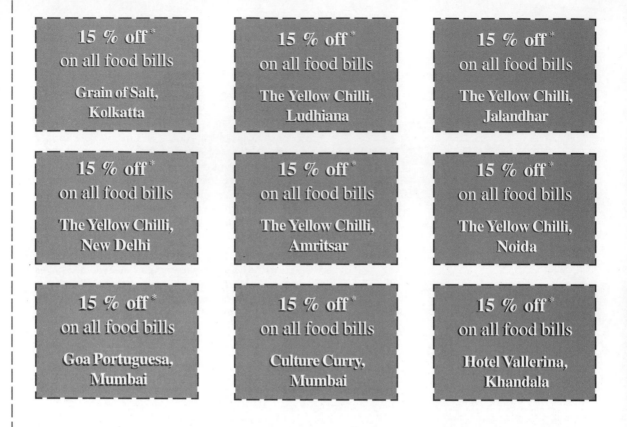

Here's a chance to eat to your heart's content…that too at a fabulous discount.
Simply cut the coupons above and present them at any of the nine restaurants mentioned below.

1. Grain of Salt, Camac Street, Kolkatta.
2. The Yellow Chilly, Sarabha Nagar, Ludhiana.
3. The Yellow Chilly, Restaurant of Hotel Residency, near Bus Stand, Jalandhar.
4. The Yellow Chilly, Pitampura, New Delhi.
5. The Yellow Chilli, Basant Avenue, Amritsar.
6. The Yellow Chilli, Sector 18, Atta Market, Noida.
7. Goa Portuguesa, Mahim, Mumbai.
8. Culture Curry, Mahim, Mumbai.
9. Hotel Vallerina, Khandala.

* Conditions apply